TYPO3 4.2 E-Commerce

Design, build, and profit from a sophisticated
feature-rich online store using TYPO3

Inese Liberte

Edgars Karlsons

BIRMINGHAM - MUMBAI

TYPO3 4.2 E-Commerce

First published: April 2010

Production Reference: 1230410

Published by Packt Publishing Ltd.
32 Lincoln Road
Olton
Birmingham, B27 6PA, UK.

ISBN 978-1-847198-52-5

www.packtpub.com

Cover Image by Karl Moore (karl.moore@ukonline.co.uk)

Credits

Authors
Inese Liberte
Edgars Karlsons

Reviewers
Ingo Schmitt
Peter Proll
Simon Browning

Acquisition Editor
Rashmi Phadnis

Development Editor
Neha Patwari

Technical Editor
Ajay Shanker

Copy Editor
Lakshmi Menon

Editorial Team Leader
Akshara Aware

Project Team Leader
Lata Basantani

Project Coordinator
Poorvi Nair

Proofreader
Aaron Nash

Indexer
Rekha Nair

Production Coordinator
Adline Swetha Jesuthas

Cover Work
Adline Swetha Jesuthas

About the Authors

Inese Liberte is an entrepreneur from Latvia with more than 10 years experience in IT. She has been professionally involved in areas such as information processing, data analysis, visual applications, and process management.

Since her studies at the gymnasium, the author has a deep interest in the natural sciences, technologies, IT, and programming. This is reflected in her professional pursuits too. One of her professional experiences was giving lectures on the topic of using MS Office in the fields of economics and accounting. The teaching experience not only gave professional insights, but also revealed the different ways in which people perceive IT, learn, and use it. This experience was relevant for developing various projects, including IT projects, data analysis, and telecommunication projects.

Creativity, communication skills, and positive thinking are among the main characteristics of Inese Liberte. One of her greatest experiences was working with a leading Latvian news portal.

She also writes poetry and many of her poems have been published. In 2006, her book "Dream... Life" was published, which is a collection of more than 40 different stories about people's dreams, ideas, and their realizations.

The knowledge of IT and the creative part of Inese is the basis for entrepreneurial activities where she develops ideas and offers services that are dynamically adjusted to the specific needs of the customers.

Since 2008, Inese Liberte is the co-owner of private enterprise "Netberries", which specializes in developing web pages on the basis of TYPO3 CMS. The company has managed to find its specific approach to clients by both ensuring functionality of a web page and adjusting it to a custom design. There is a positive feedback from the customers about the technical development of the web pages, the maintenance, consulting, and also customer services.

The author's leading notion in the field of technologies is creativity—that it is possible to attach an edge of individuality even to the rigid technological process. Therefore, it is important to dare to experiment and to search for new opportunities.

I would like to express gratitude to my family and friends for supporting me during the writing of this book. Special thanks to Mārtiņš Liberts (IT, "TietoEnator Alise", Latvia) and Reinis Rotkalis (graphic design, "Give Us Work", Latvia).

Also, we would like to say thanks to Packt Publishing for the great chance to write this book, to Poorvi, to our reviewers — Ingo and Simon, and to our editors — Neha Patwari and Rashmi for valuable advice. And many thanks to all our readers — you are the reason we wrote this book.

Edgars Karlson has worked for more than seven years in the field of web development. He started as a freelancer but over the years he has improved his profession in both providing a quality service and also in pursuit of new technological solutions. Along with web solutions, Edgars has worked with web graphics and applications programming.

Along with IT project management, Edgars Karlsons has gained some teaching experience — he has given seminars on using specific technological products, on transmitting packet data, and working with several application programs. He has also gained experience in practical psychology, which is of also great use in the field of IT, when a complicated problem has to be solved.

The management skills of Edgars Karlsons have improved during his career — from leading small interest groups to managing large international IT projects. One of his most important professional notions is high precision.

In 2006, Edgars Karlsons saw the creative potentiality in TYPO3 CMS. This resulted in establishing a private enterprise that specializes in developing web pages basing on TYPO3 CMS.

Netberries Ltd. has been successful for several years; it has developed JSON (JavaScript Object Notation) based applications, custom jQuery scripts, and xHTML/CSS websites. Since 2008, the company has been working with TYPO3 CMS. Netberries installs TYPO3 websites, creates the design, trains the clients, and provides maintenance.

Recently, the company has started development of TYPO3 extensions. There is an in-house team of IT specialists, but outsourcing is also used.

Edgars Karlsons saw writing this book about creating an online shop as a challenge to his skills and knowledge about TYPO3 systems.

This project certainly would not be possible without the official TYPO3 mailing list—thanks for the help! I would like to express gratitude to my family that has supported me throughout my life, thus giving me the opportunity to write this book.

Special thanks to my dog Zhannah who was especially patient and understanding while her master was writing this book and thus was not able to play with her. Likewise, thanks to my friends from Miera street Crew and also to one very special person, who has given me loads of motivation to work hard and strive for success.

About the Reviewers

Ingo Schmitt, was born in 1974, studied Electrical Engineering at the 'Universität Gesamthochschule Duisburg', Germany, learned Pascal, C++, discovered the Web with Netscape 1.0, and started working for Marketing Factory Consulting GmbH, Düsseldorf in 1996. Working with PHP, he developed web-based applications, releasing his first extranet online shop in 1998. As the CTO of Marketing Factory Consulting GmbH, he started working with TYPO3 in 2002, including developing his own extensions. Ingo Schmitt is the founder and main developer of TYPO3 Commerce, TYPO3 Certified Engineer, and 'IHK Prüfer für Fachinformatiker'.

Marketing Factory Consulting GmbH is one of the top TYPO3 Agencies in Germany, developing Web and Portal applications for clients such as Henkel, Ista, Metabo, Wrigley, and Westfalia. Marketing Factory also runs its own websites, such as heimwerker.de (the biggest DIY site in German language), ratgeber.de, and online shops like blumenbutler.de.

Simon Browning is the founder of SeeThrough Web (www.seethroughweb.com), a Toronto, Canada-based web design and hosting company that serves a wide range of clients throughout the small to medium-sized business community, and also provides development services to design and marketing agencies.

With 15 years of information technology experience, including managing the Canadian Information Systems group of a large multi-national, Simon is of the attitude "get it done right, get it done on-time, and keep it simple". This attitude was a guiding factor in the selection of TYPO3 as SeeThrough Web's preferred and recommended content management system. Since 2005, SeeThrough Web has used TYPO3 in over 100 client projects, ranging from small corporate websites to high traffic online portals.

Table of Contents

Preface

The popularity of online shopping has increased drastically over the past few years. TYPO3 is fully equipped to meet all the challenges of modern electronic commerce. TYPO3 can be enlarged from a pure content-based online catalog to a fully-grown shop system with a variety of extensions.

It may be easy to plan a website but when it comes to implementing the design and developing a successful e-Commerce site, you might come across a lot of difficulties.

This book teaches all the aspects of quickly setting up a feature-packed, easy-to-build e-Commerce site—from basic installation and configuration of TYPO3, through adding features step-by-step to an example website. It demonstrates the setting up of an online TYPO3 e-Commerce site from scratch and walks you through lucrative tips on attracting customers and maximizing profit.

This book takes you through the creation of an appealing online shop in steps. It starts with the basics of TYPO3 and TYPO3 installation and shows you how to use its standard features to begin construction of an online shop. It will help you improve the selling interface and handling of orders with new modules and other customizations. It discusses various template configurations and plugins. You will learn how to build attractive product catalogs, profiles for registered and unregistered users, and online shop SEO. You will also learn to provide effective search facilities for systematic navigation of your site. Further, various modules for payment and delivery will be discussed. Finally, you will learn how to manage and market your site.

This book is a step-by-step, instruction-packed tutorial that teaches you to build a TYPO3 e-Commerce website through practical examples.

What This Book Covers

Chapter 1, TYPO3 Installation and Extension Selection explains how to install TYPO3 and choose the appropriate extension.

Chapter 2, Template Configuration describes the TYPO3 template configuration. Using TYPO3, you can set up templates in the same way as for statistical HTML web pages.

Chapter 3, Singularity of TYPO3 E-Commerce Plugins describes the TYPO3 e-Commerce plugins you can use to provide a payment possibility in your online shop. Also, we will describe the most popular payments, such as online and offline payments using a card and the PayPal system, which is the most popular form of payment at the moment.

Chapter 4, Catalogue - Setting Up Online Shop Requirements describes the requirements for setting up an online shop, explaining how to set up a catalogue of products, how to prepare product-descriptive information (images and textual information), and how to organize the structure of the catalogue.

Chapter 5, Shop Users - Profiles for Unregistered and Registered Users describes the organization of unregistered and registered users, and how to add features for advanced users' options.

Chapter 6, Navigation Inside the Online Shop and Content Search describes navigation and searching possibilities inside shop content. This chapter also describes how to organize common, supplementary, and linked content navigation.

Chapter 7, Ordering Organization - Modules of Payment and Delivery describes how to add modules of payment and delivery for ordering and buying products.

Chapter 8, Administrative Interface in TYPO3 describes the possibilities of administrating shop content using the administrative interface in TYPO3 backend.

Chapter 9, Online Shop SEO Development describes online shop web page optimization corresponding to SEO requirements, and explains how to increase web presence on search engines.

Chapter 10, Managing and Marketing Your Site describes the most important aspects for managing and marketing the site.

Who this book is for

If you want to create a captivating online shop using TYPO3 and optimize your profit, this book is for you. Some knowledge of TYPO3, PHP, and TypoScript is required.

Conventions

In this book, you will find a number of styles of text that distinguish between different kinds of information. Here are some examples of these styles, and an explanation of their meaning.

Code words in text are shown as follows: "We can include other contexts through the use of the `include` directive."

A block of code will be set as follows:

```
<div class="menu">###MENU###</div>
<div class="left-col">###LEFTCOL###</div>
<div class="main-cont">###MAINCONT###</div>
<div class="footer">###FOOTER###</div>
```

New terms and **important words** are introduced in a bold-type font. Words that you see on the screen, in menus or dialog boxes for example, appear in our text like this: "clicking the **Next** button moves you to the next screen".

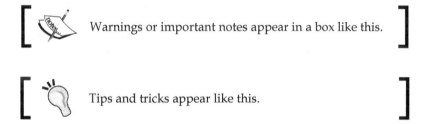

Warnings or important notes appear in a box like this.

Tips and tricks appear like this.

Reader Feedback

Feedback from our readers is always welcome. Let us know what you think about this book, what you liked or may have disliked. Reader feedback is important for us to develop titles that you really get the most out of.

To send us general feedback, simply drop an email to `feedback@packtpub.com`, making sure to mention the book title in the subject of your message.

If there is a book that you need and would like to see us publish, please send us a note in the **SUGGEST A TITLE** form on `www.packtpub.com` or email `suggest@packtpub.com`.

If there is a topic that you have expertise in and you are interested in either writing or contributing to a book, see our author guide on `www.packtpub.com/authors`.

Customer Support

Now that you are the proud owner of a Packt book, we have a number of things to help you to get the most from your purchase.

Errata

Although we have taken every care to ensure the accuracy of our contents, mistakes do happen. If you find a mistake in one of our books — maybe a mistake in text or code — we would be grateful if you would report this to us. By doing this you can save other readers from frustration, and help to improve subsequent versions of this book. If you find any errata, report them by visiting `http://www.packtpub.com/support`, selecting your book, clicking on the **let us know** link, and entering the details of your errata. Once your errata are verified, your submission will be accepted and the errata added to the list of existing errata. The existing errata can be viewed by selecting your title from `http://www.packtpub.com/support`.

Piracy

Piracy of copyright material on the Internet is an ongoing problem across all media. At Packt, we take the protection of our copyright and licenses very seriously. If you come across any illegal copies of our works in any form on the Internet, please provide the location address or website name immediately so we can pursue a remedy.

Please contact us at `copyright@packtpub.com` with a link to the suspected pirated material.

We appreciate your help in protecting our authors, and our ability to bring you valuable content.

Questions

You can contact us at `questions@packtpub.com` if you are having a problem with some aspect of the book, and we will do our best to address it.

1
TYPO3 Installation and Extension Selection

TYPO3 is one of the most functional and powerful content management systems (CMS). Offering both functionality and expansiveness, TYPO3 is a relevant competitor for commercial solutions. Considering that there are thousands of extensions available at the moment ("plugins" are called extensions in the TYPO3 community), this chapter explains how to install TYPO3 and choose the appropriate extension. The topics covered here include:

- Ways to install TYPO3
- Extension installation

By the end of this chapter, you will have installed TYPO3 for a particular domain.

Installation of TYPO3

TYPO3 is developed and is in use as GNU General Public License (a free, copyleft license for non-profit and commercial homepages). This software was created in 1997 and is still being supplemented with new functions. The basic server requirements are:

- A web server with Apache (recommended) — Apache (under Linux, Windows, Unix platforms) or IIS (under Windows platform)
- PHP — TYPO3 version 4.2 onwards; you need a PHP 5.2 or higher
- MySQL database

These server extras are also recommended:

- GraphicsMagick (standalone). ImageMagick will work too.
- GDlib/Freetype (compiled with PHP).
- zlib (compiled with PHP).
- Apache with `mod_gzip`/`mod_rewrite`.
- A PHP-cache (for example, PHP-accelerator/Zend Accelerator, Unix only).

There are a few basic steps to start your first TYPO3-driven shop:

1. First, you need a copy of TYPO3. In this example, we used the dummy and core package that is needed for a new installation. You can get your free copy at `http://typo3.org/download`.

If you prefer using the SSH/Shell Access (especially in a Unix server), we recommend downloading the `*.tgz` package. This package contains symbolic links (symlinks). If you use a Unix server with the ability to create symlinks, download the `*.tgz` package.

You will find detailed information about TYPO3 installation on different servers at TYPO3Wiki: `http://wiki.typo3.org/index.php/TYPO3_Installation_Basics`

2. Choose one of the installer packages if you don't have a web server, or choose the zip or `tar.gz` packages option if you do have a web server.

3. Unzip the copy of TYPO3 with a decompressing software such as WinZip, WinRar, or 7Zip—the choice is up to you.

4. Upload a copy of TYPO3 to your FTP web space with the accordant FTP software. To start the installation you need to add an extra file—the `ENABLE_INSTALL_TOOL`. You have to create this file independently. For example, you could create the file `ENABLE_INSTALL_TOOL.txt` and upload this file to your TYPO3 installation folder `/TYPO3-ROOT-FOLDER/typo3conf`. Then, delete the file extension `*.txt`.

To be safe, we recommend FileZilla and the SFTP mode if possible.

Base requirements for different operational systems and installation in different operational systems' environments are described on the TYPO3Wiki page: `http://wiki.typo3.org/index.php/TYPO3_Installation_Basics`. You could also go to the TYPO3 homepage: `http://typo3.org/documentation/document-library/extension-manuals/doc_basicinstall/current/`.

You can run the TYPO3 Install tool now.

Installing TYPO3

In the following section, we cover the installation of TYPO3 using the TYPO3 Install tool.

TYPO3 Install tool

You can use the 1-2-3 Install tool, which has three simple steps, to install TYPO3 on your hosting server.

To access the TYPO3 Install tool, open your web page: `http://[yoursitename. com]/index.php` and you will be redirected to the **TYPO3 1-2-3 install** script that provides an easy setup of TYPO3.

The default password is `joh316`. It is recommended that you change this password after the installation is complete. The following is a screenshot of the installation start-up:

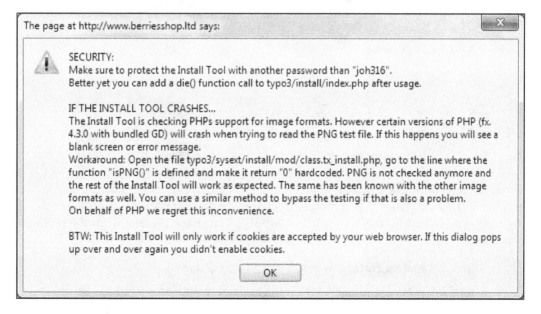

The page at http://www.berriesshop.ltd says:

SECURITY:
Make sure to protect the Install Tool with another password than "joh316".
Better yet you can add a die() function call to typo3/install/index.php after usage.

IF THE INSTALL TOOL CRASHES...
The Install Tool is checking PHPs support for image formats. However certain versions of PHP (fx. 4.3.0 with bundled GD) will crash when trying to read the PNG test file. If this happens you will see a blank screen or error message.
Workaround: Open the file typo3/sysext/install/mod/class.tx_install.php, go to the line where the function "isPNG()" is defined and make it return "0" hardcoded. PNG is not checked anymore and the rest of the Install Tool will work as expected. The same has been known with the other image formats as well. You can use a similar method to bypass the testing if that is also a problem.
On behalf of PHP we regret this inconvenience.

BTW: This Install Tool will only work if cookies are accepted by your web browser. If this dialog pops up over and over again you didn't enable cookies.

OK

The TYPO3 1-2-3 Install tool allows you, in three simple steps, to connect to the MySQL database and import the default tables from the database dump file. You can choose to create a new database and add tables to the main database. There were 36 tables in our installation for version 4.2.8.

Database access information

Using a hosting service can often lead to a situation where you need to create a database independently using the Control Panel tools. For example, if you use cPanel for creating a new database, you need to:

1. Authorize in Control Panel.
2. Go to the section **Databases** and select **MySQL Databases**.
3. Enter the name of the new database.
4. Click on the **Create Database** button.

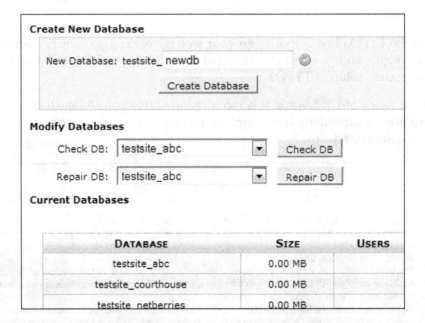

If you create a database this way, you should add the previously created user account to this database. If you choose to create the database and user account together, you have to select the function **MySQL Database Wizard** from the section **Databases**. This wizard contains the following steps:

1. **Step 1: Create a Database** (enter the database name).
2. **Step 2: Create Database user** (enter username and password for user).

3. **Step 3: Add user to the Database** (enable/disable user database privileges such as insert, edit, delete, and drop, among others). We recommend choosing **All privileges** in the checkbox for normal TYPO3 installation.

4. **Step 4: Complete the task**. After these four steps, you can choose to return to the first page of admin tool, create another database, or create additional user accounts for the database.

This is Step 1 in the TYPO3 installation. Write the database access information in the respective fields—username and password. After this, approve the information and move onto the next step:

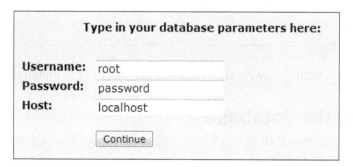

Here, enter the username and password to access your database:

- **Username** — given username
- **Password** — given password
- **Host** — often "localhost"

Choosing a database

This is Step 2 in the installation of TYPO3. With this step, you can choose the existent database or create a new one (recommended). Usually, hosting service providers offer already created databases wherein you won't have permissions to create a new one.

It is different if you use a website hosting service that allows managing your web space or if you are the web server administrator; then, you may be able to create a new database through the TYPO3 Install script.

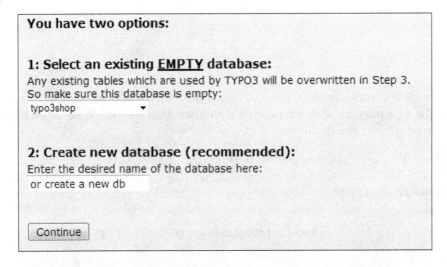

Select an existing database or create a new one for the TYPO3 installation.

Importing the database

This is Step 3 in the installation of TYPO3. Import the database SQL file by pressing the **Import database** button.

After these three steps, you are done with TYPO3's basic installation.

For a complete installation, you should continue with the configuration—also called **Normal** mode, which secures additional options for TYPO3's complete functionality. Here you can continue page configuration, providing the preferred page operations. Using the section *Basic Configuration*, you can activate and set up the following:

- ImageMagick or GraphicsMagick: for processing images (for TYPO3 image resizing, cropping, and special effects). If you choose ImageMagick, specify its location on the web server (in case ImageMagick is installed in the "non standard" folder and TYPO3 can't find it).

- GDLib: options for text processing and converting it to an image.

- TTF font size: 72 or 96 (look at the generated image—if it fits the box, you can leave it at size 72, or you can set it to 96).

- Format of image generation: take note that the *.png format files are more qualitative than the *.gif files. The maximum color scale of a *.gif file's is only 256 colors.

Configuring your TYPO3 installation

To switch to Normal mode, click on the link at the bottom of the TYPO3 Install tool. You will be able to configure the content management system in detail in the Normal mode. The following screenshot shows the configuration of TYPO3 settings:

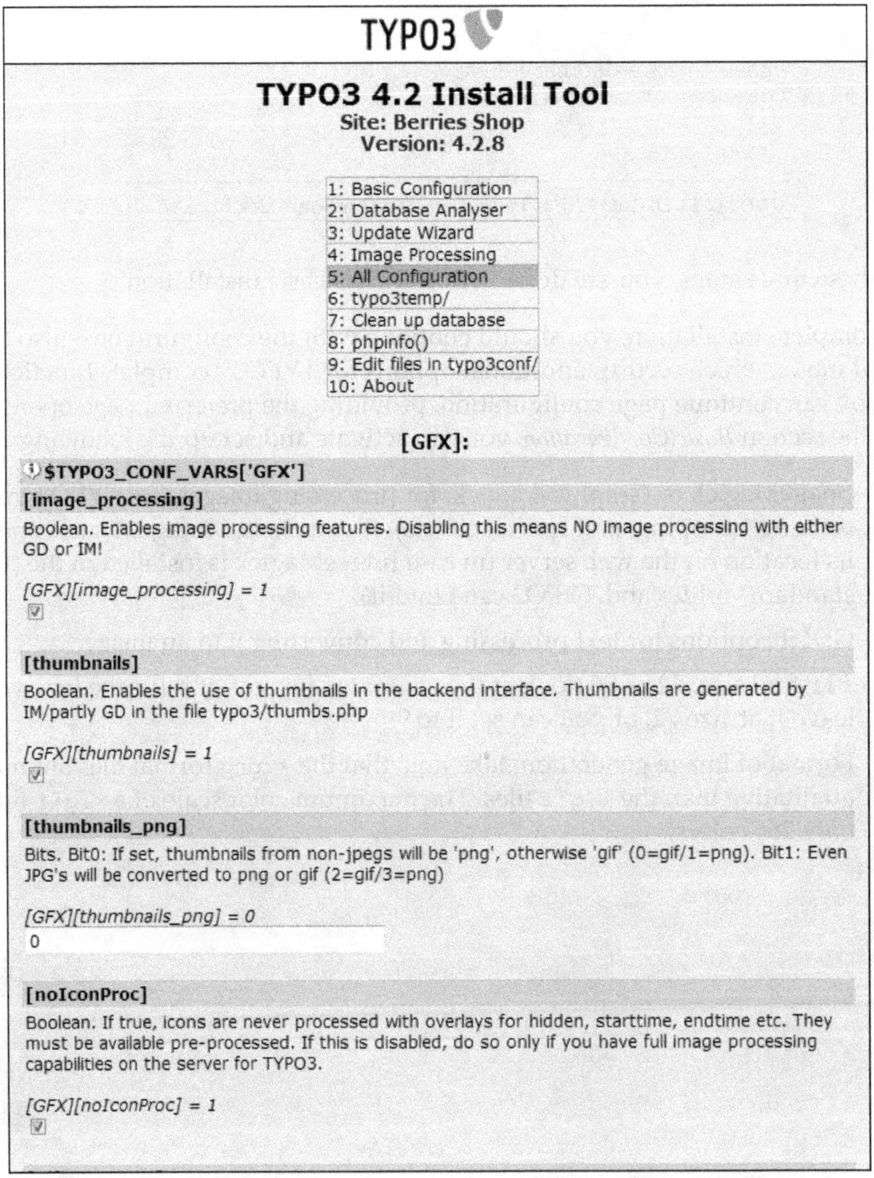

TYPO3

TYPO3 4.2 Install Tool
Site: Berries Shop
Version: 4.2.8

1: Basic Configuration
2: Database Analyser
3: Update Wizard
4: Image Processing
5: All Configuration
6: typo3temp/
7: Clean up database
8: phpinfo()
9: Edit files in typo3conf/
10: About

[GFX]:

$TYPO3_CONF_VARS['GFX']

[image_processing]

Boolean. Enables image processing features. Disabling this means NO image processing with either GD or IM!

[GFX][image_processing] = 1
☑

[thumbnails]

Boolean. Enables the use of thumbnails in the backend interface. Thumbnails are generated by IM/partly GD in the file typo3/thumbs.php

[GFX][thumbnails] = 1
☑

[thumbnails_png]

Bits. Bit0: If set, thumbnails from non-jpegs will be 'png', otherwise 'gif' (0=gif/1=png). Bit1: Even JPG's will be converted to png or gif (2=gif/3=png)

[GFX][thumbnails_png] = 0
0

[noIconProc]

Boolean. If true, icons are never processed with overlays for hidden, starttime, endtime etc. They must be available pre-processed. If this is disabled, do so only if you have full image processing capabilities on the server for TYPO3.

[GFX][noIconProc] = 1
☑

We adjusted only a few points in our example that are related to image processing using GDLib and ImageMagick.

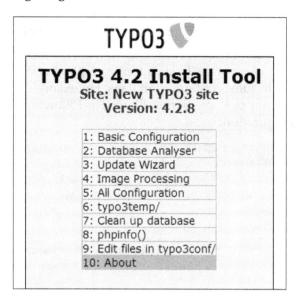

You can access **Basic Configuration**, **All Configuration**, and other useful, extra functions from here.

You can check your TYPO3 installation with basic settings at the section **Basic Configuration**:

- Do directories have enough rights to write/read content from them? If not, you should CHMOD them in the command line (in Unix systems) or by using the chosen FTP software. You can set up marketable Install tool values. For maximum safety of your installation, please read the security actions described in the TYPO3 Security Cookbook. You can find information about this book at the TYPO3 homepage: http://typo3.org/teams/security/resources/.

- php.ini configuration check: usually, you will not be able to edit this file if you're not the administrator of the hosting space.
  If your hosting administrator has granted access to some php.ini settings, you can overwrite some functions with the .htaccess file. For example, you can set the 'memory_limit', if it isn't enough, in your .htaccess file by adding an extra line:

  ```
  php_value memory_limit 64M
  ```

- GDLib and FreeType check: if there is a GDLib installed on your server and also format support check for GIF and PNG.

- ImageMagick check: checks the available installation of IM on your server. If the Install tool doesn't find it, it doesn't mean that you don't have it. We set the full path to IM by ourselves in our example.

- Basic database check: connection settings and credentials.

- Write configuration to `localconf.php`: add the needed values for site configuration and press the Update localconf.php button. Also, here you can make changes to some configuration flags. For example, give a name to your site. We called our example Berries Shop. The following screenshot shows the basic configuration:

step you will configure TYPO3 for immediate use provided that you have no fatal errors left above.

Username:	root
Password:	password
Host:	localhost
Database:	typo3shop ▾
	Create database? (Enter name):
Site name:	Berries Shop
Encryption key:	38d551bbcef94bec6e:
	Generate random key
[BE][disable_exec_function]=	0
	current value is 0
[GFX][gdlib]=	1
	current value is 1
[GFX][gdlib_png]=	0 (GIF)
	current value is 1
	1 (PNG) ▾

Settings at localconf.php file

System's options are stored in the `localconf.php` (`/typo3conf/localconf.php`) file. If necessary, you can edit and complement options manually using one of the text editors. We added the following values:

```
$TYPO3_CONF_VARS['GFX']['im'] = '1';
```

describes that we will use ImageMagick.

```
$TYPO3_CONF_VARS['GFX']['gdlib_2'] = '1';
```

enables the usage of GDLib2 (if applicable).

```
$TYPO3_CONF_VARS['GFX']['im_version_5'] = 'im6';
```

we're using ImageMagick v.6, so we entered `im6`.

You can set this flag depending on the version of ImageMagick that you use. Values can be `im4`, `im5`, `im6`, or `gm` (if you need to use GraphicsMagick instead of IM).

```
$TYPO3_CONF_VARS['GFX']['gdlib_png'] = '1';
```

set at `1` to generate text as images in PNG format. Also, you can leave this value at `0` to keep it in GIF format.

```
$TYPO3_CONF_VARS['GFX']['im_imvMaskState'] = '1';
```

inverts the state of `im_negate_mask` if set.

```
$TYPO3_CONF_VARS['GFX']['im_v5effects'] = '1';
```

this setting allows creating blur or sharpening effects. If set, it cancels the `im_no_effects` flag.

```
$TYPO3_CONF_VARS['BE']['installToolPassword']
='0c6ca3b2c0891c8a74026cf1743148e8';
```

sets the Install Tool password `berriesshop` (md5 hashed). You can set it at the **About** section, or if necessary, create the md5 hash by yourself.

```
$TYPO3_CONF_VARS['BE']['forceCharset'] = 'utf-8';
```

by default, the TYPO3 administration panel is called **Backend** and has charset iso-8859-1, but we switched it to `utf-8`.

After these changes, save your `localconf.php` file and upload it to the web server.

Now you can log into the administration panel (backend) with the default username `admin` and password `password`.

To be safe do the following:

- Change the default password for the user `admin` (at the backend section **User settings**).
- Change the TYPO3 Install tool password (at the **About** section of the Install Tools).
- Delete the `ENABLE_INSTALL_TOOL` file (`/typo3conf/ENABLE_INSTALL_TOOL`) from `web space/web server`.

- Also, you'll be informed about the undone security operations when you
  log into the TYPO3 backend. More important security aspects are described
  in the *TYPO3 Security Cookbook*. You can find it at the TYPO3 homepage:
  `http://typo3.org/teams/security/resources/`.

Installing TYPO3 extensions

One of the advantages of using TYPO3 is that this CMS has expandability
possibilities that are called "extensions". Using these extensions, you can extend
the TYPO3 functionality. You can manage shops, galleries, forums, or even a small
community portal.

You can download extensions from the TYPO3 extension repository (TER):
`http://typo3.org/extensions`.
`*.t3x` is the file format used for extension files. This package is partly compressed
using GZIP and it contains the necessary files for the extension (SQL dump, tables,
functions, templates, image resources, and so on). This site is a recommended
easy way to search for appropriate and suitable extensions. Also, you can find an
overview of the extension functionality and additional documentation. For easy
extension installation, use its import through Extension Manager.

In the extensions section, `http://typo3.org/extensions`, you'll find the following:

- **New and updated**: the latest updated or recently added extensions from
  the last 20 days—as per the claim on the repository.

- **Popular**: a list of the most downloaded extensions on TER.

- **Full list**: a complete list of extensions sorted by alphabet.

- **Search**: search the form to find an appropriate extension you need.
  A Search form is also provided in the section **New and updated**.

All the extensions are sorted in groups according to their status:

- **Reviewed extensions**: extensions that are secure. These extensions don't
  affect the normal operation of the system and are qualitative.

- **Alfa**: early stage of extension development.

- **Beta**: early stage of extension development but operates partly.

- **Stable**: stable extension that can be used to provide page functionality.

- **Test**: test extension. These kinds of extensions are usually without
  functionality or are used for concept examples.

- **Obsolete**: extensions that are included in the TYPO3 core or are associated
  with other extensions.

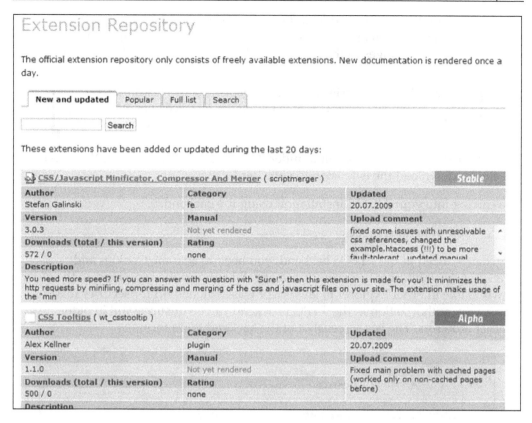

For our new shop, we need an eCommerce extension that provides product catalogue and functionality of a shopping cart. You can type shop or commerce in the search area and get a few versions of online shop extensions and those extensions that provide extra functionality to basic extensions.

Note the most popular and downloaded online shop extensions:

- Shop System (tt_products) by Franz Holzinger
- Webformat Shop System (extendedshop) by Mauro Lorenzutti
- Commerce (commerce) by Ingo Schmitt, Volker Graubaum, and Thomas Hempel

The difference between these extensions is the functionality. For our online shop creation, we chose tt_products. This extension is updated, well-documented, has a lot of nice features, and has flexible configuration possibilities.

You can click on the extension title and find the basic information about the extension: the author, the updated date and version, a link to the manual, information about changes in the current version, decryptions, and dependencies.

 Not all extensions can work together. For this reason, always compare extensions with the already installed ones. Also, we recommend comparing used TYPO3 versions of extensions.

There is an available download link under the extension's description. You can use this link to download the extension to your hard drive.

You can log into your TYPO3 installation using the backend:

`http://www.yourdomain.com/typo3.`

To get authorized in the TYPO3 backend, you need to activate Cookies and JavaScript. New Internet browsers automatically support these options. In the older browsers like Internet Explorer 6, JavaScript was switched off for security reasons. This is why authorization in the TYPO3 backend can be unsuccessful in older Internet browsers. The is a screenshot of the backend login form:

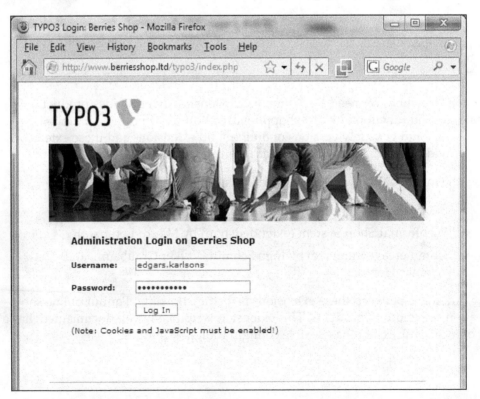

Type in the username and password. The default username is `admin` and the password is `password`. After you are logged on, for security reasons change the password by clicking on the link in the warning window or in the section **User Admin**:

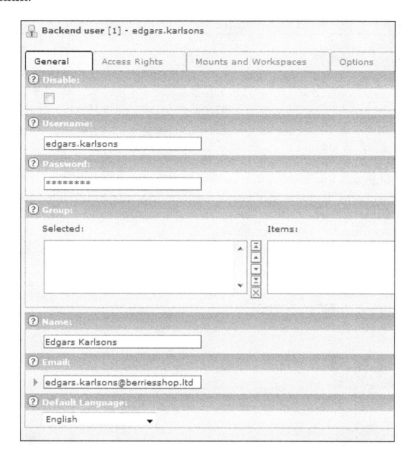

Change the username `admin` and password to your chosen identification data. You can enter a name, e-mail, and preferred language, and save the data by clicking on the **Save and close document** button.

After the identification data are changed, update the reference index by clicking on
Update Reference Index.

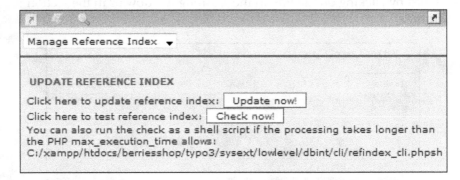

You could get to this function from the main backend page or choose it from the side
menu in the section **DB check**. Choose the section **Manage Reference Index** and
click on the **Update Now!** button. The following screenshot shows the **Extension
Manager** in the BE administration panel:

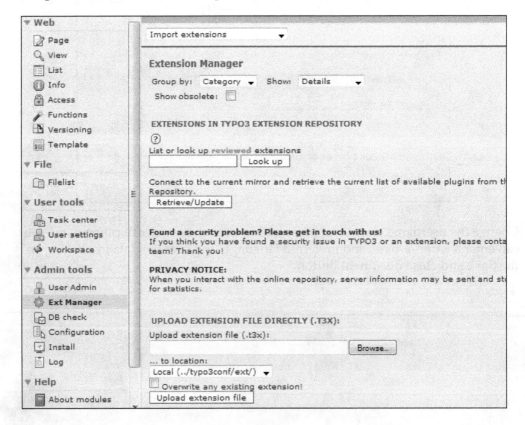

For extensions imported to TYPO3, use the Extension Manager. Choose **Import Extensions** from the drop-down menu at the top. The easiest way to install new extensions is to use the function at the top of the module under **List of look up reviewed/all extensions**. Hit the **Retrieve/Update** button to get a list with the updated extensions and enter the necessary extension name, for example "tt_products".

The extension will not be found if it isn't "reviewed". For switching this off, choose **Settings** from the drop-down menu, and check **Enable extensions without review (basic security check)** under **Security Settings**.

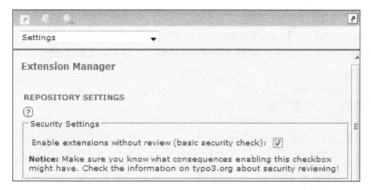

Now go back to the section **Import Extensions**. First, update the list of extensions by clicking on **Retrieve/Update**. When the list update is complete, in the search field type the extension name — in our case "tt_products".

In the search results you would find the extension **tt_products** and extensions that have a similar name or description:

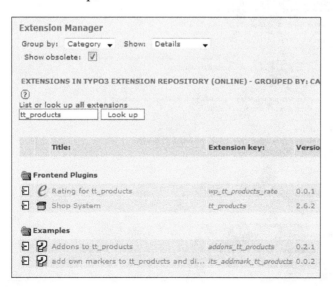

Press the import button with the red arrow for the extension import to your web server. After the import is successfully done, you can go on to the extension installation.

Now press the **+** icon for **Install extension**. The following screenshot shows the extension installation step with the data import in the database:

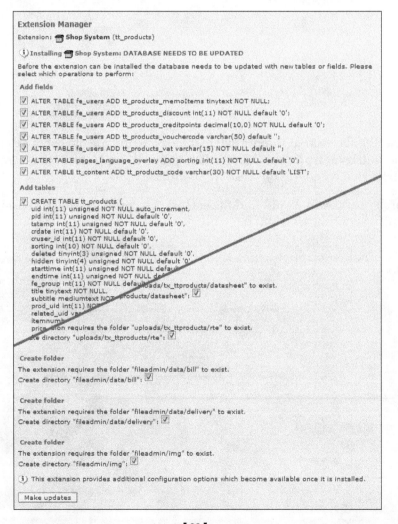

Click on the **Make updates** button, and the extension will automatically add new tables and a new upload folder `tx_ttproducts` with subfolders (for product images, datasheets, rich text editor (RTE), and bills). The following screenshot shows the additional settings for extension:

```
Extension Manager
Extension:  Shop System (tt_products)

 ACTIVE STATUS:

The extension is installed (loaded and running)!
Click here to remove the extension: 

 CONFIGURATION:

(Notice: You may need to clear the cache after configuration of the extension. This is required if the extension adds T

Enable features
  Use Page as Category [pageAsCategory]
  If you want to use the pages as categories and the categories as subcategories. =1: the pages
  completely replace the categories =2
  [0                                                                    ]


  Use Flexforms [useFlexforms]
  Enable the use of Flexforms in the backend. Extension fh_library version 0.0.12+ must be installed.
  Default is 1.
  [✓]


  Use patch 1822 [usePatch1822]
  Install this patch from bugs.typo3.org to have an advanced page module
  [ ]


[ Update ]
```

After the extension is installed, you can choose extra options or leave the default settings. We recommend leaving Flexforms. For using Flexforms, you don't have the additional install extension `fh_library` that is needed only for `tt_products` versions 2.5.2-2.6.0.

Also, we require the extension `Table Library (table)` for the extension tt_products.

All the extensions are available at TYPO3 TER. For better search results, you can write the full extension title or part of it—for example, 'Static Methods' (without quotes).

The tt_products dependencies that are compulsory for the operation of the extension (at the time of writing this book) are:

- "Shop System" — tt_products, version: 2.6.2
- "Static Methods for Extensions since 2007" — div2007, version: 0.2.4
- "Table Library" — table, version: 0.1.32

Summary

TYPO3 is one of the most functional and powerful content management systems. For comprehensive system functionality, we require a definite server power and an accordant software. The TYPO3 1-2-3 Install tool allows you, in three simple steps, to connect to the MySQL database and import the default tables from the database dump file. After these three steps, you are done with the TYPO3 basic installation that will provide the main functionality. For a complete installation, you should switch to advanced, also called "Normal" mode, which secures additional options for the complete functionality of TYPO3. Using extensions, you can extend the TYPO3 functionality.

In the next chapter, we will describe the TYPO3 template configuration. Using TYPO3, you can set up templates in the same way as for statistical HTML web pages.

2
Template Configuration

This chapter shows you how to configure the designed template, and discusses the most frequently encountered issues. It also shows you how to upgrade TYPO3 to a newer version. The topics covered are:

- TYPO3 script configuration
- Template markers
- Manual template adding
- Upgrading to a newer version

By the end of this chapter, you will know the difference between the two types of templates—the TypoScript configuration templates and the HTML layout templates—and you will have added design into the TYPO3 CMS. It is useful to follow the TYPO3 CMS updates. So, this chapter explains how to upgrade your web page to newer version of TYPO3.

Configuring templates to add design

For TYPO3, you can use templates in the same way as for all web pages and for more well-known content management systems. There are several kinds of templates already developed that you can use, or you can develop your own template.

It is an important fact that for making an HTML template for your TYPO3 web page, you need to have a basic knowledge of HTML and TYPO3-specific configuration—**TypoScript**. However, you don't have to know PHP.

Types of templates

TypoScript is a powerful configuration language used in TYPO3. TypoScript isn't a programming language, it is a configuration language that provides output for already-programmed functions. With TypoScript, you can't program new functions.

Most of TypoScript configuration is related to creating templates, but you can also use TypoScript for other configurations. For example, with TypoScript you can configure the column amount in the backend, view of RTE (Rich Text Editor), and available functions, among others.

The TypoScript template is composed of several parts:

- Constants part—where values are fixed for repeatable use and extension setups.
- Setup part—this is the configuration for template, menus, h1 tag replacement with graphical image, and so on.

You can also use added resources as templates for your online shop. For example, you can use HTML templates. You need to use a template system so that you can organize or locate your web page content. After setting up the template, you can check the content layout and content view. You can choose the template you want to use. Templates can have one or more columns, with or without a header and footer.

If you are using TYPO3, you can select from several options: using prepared templates, developing a template on your own, using templates with a commercial license and adapting it for TYPO3, and so on.

Templates can be divided into basic types:

- **Default static templates**: Templates that are already in the TYPO3 package, for example, BUSINESS, CANDIDATE, FIRST, GREEN, HYPER, and so on. You don't need to have any extra skills and knowledge for using these templates, but they have limited capabilities. Using the default templates, it is possible to attain the web page functionality that you need. Using your own templates allows you to make the web page more suitable for page requirements.

- **HTML templates (modern template building)**: This is the kind of template you need to create for your custom template; also, you need to set up the custom TypoScript configuration. This method is similar to the Smarty template system where you use markers for creating templates, but this similarity is partial. Here you need to add markers in the created template, whereas in Smarty added content will be generated. Using TypoScript, you need to specify the kind of content that will be shown in the marker's area—where the HTML template on your web server is located, what is additionally required to be included in the source (CSS, JavaScript files), and also what is outputted in the header section of the HTML document. You can find more detailed information about this template building on the TYPO3 home page: `http://typo3.org/documentation/document-library/tutorials/doc_tut_templselect/current/`.

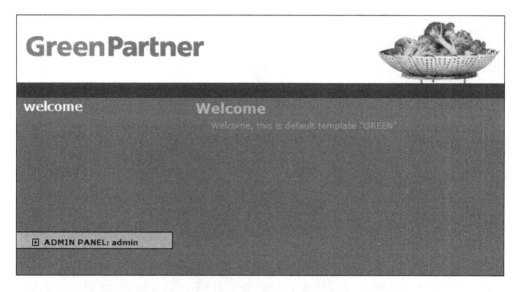

- TemplaVoila!: This is an extra extension that you can download from the TYPO3 repository. TemplaVoila! is currently developed by Dmitry Dulepov as a replacement for the normal HTML templates. Using this type of template will make it possible to add design and content in a more flexible manner.

- And a few more: For example, **Smarty**, and **automaketemplate**. Smarty and automaketemplate are TYPO3 extensions.

We used pre-developed HTML templates with the TypoScript configuration in our online shop as you'll see further.

Template development and integration

We are using the more well-known method: developing HTML templates (HTML documents) with TypoScript configuration.

Starting work with this method, you need to create a new folder for the HTML template file, for the CSS (Cascading Style Sheets) file, and for images that will be used in the developing design. We recommend creating a new folder in: [your-typo3-installation]/fileadmin/templates/

You need to create a new folder in the fileadmin folder:

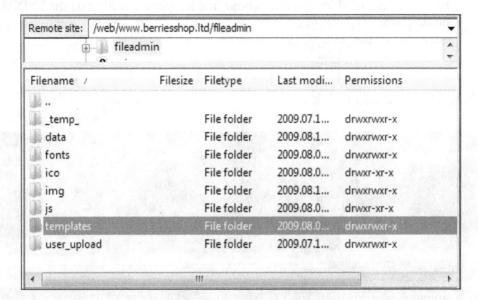

For our new online shop, we'll create one more folder (child folder) named berriesshop. If you are planning to create several templates or you feel that data arrangement and sorting will help with looking through the web page structure, you can split templates—for example, "berriesshop", "berriesshop-intranet", or "berriesshop-new-template".

As mentioned, you can set up templates in the same way as for statistical HTML web pages that you probably developed before starting to use the advantages of the content management systems.

Setting up the template, you need to include:

- Header section (will be removed and replaced with the TypoScript configuration): This section you can leave incomplete until you are creating an HTML template for the header settings local test.

- Main body content section (`<div>` tags or table-based design).

For example, you can create a template with the following structure:

```
<!DOCTYPE html PUBLIC "-//W3C//DTD XHTML 1.0 Transitional//EN"
"http://www.w3.org/TR/xhtml1/DTD/xhtml1-transitional.dtd">
<html xmlns="http://www.w3.org/1999/xhtml">
<head>
<meta http-equiv="Content-Type" content="text/html; charset=utf-8" />
<title>Document title</title>

</head>
<body>

<div class="main-container">
    <div class="header">
       <div class="logo">###LOGO###</div>
       <div class="lang-switch">###LANGUAGES###</div>
    </div>
    <div class="menu">###MENU###</div>
    <div class="left-col">###LEFTCOL###</div>
    <div class="main-cont">###MAINCONT###</div>
    <div class="footer">###FOOTER###</div>
</div>

</body>
</html>
```

There is a main `<div>` nest with child `<div>` and prepared markers for our TypoScript configuration:

`"logo"`: This will be a marker for image.

`"lang-switch"`: If you need translated content, this will be a marker for languages.

`"menu"`: This will be a marker for a top menu. Also, you can add additional markers for side menus, among others.

`"left-col"`: This will be a marker for left column content.

`"main-cont"`: This will be a marker for main content (right column).

"footer": This will be a marker for some extra information that you would like to show to your website visitors. Extra information can be copyright information, date, owner, contacts, and so on.

Also, you can add any markers that you need. These markers can be extra titles, breadcrumbs-menu, date/time, and so on.

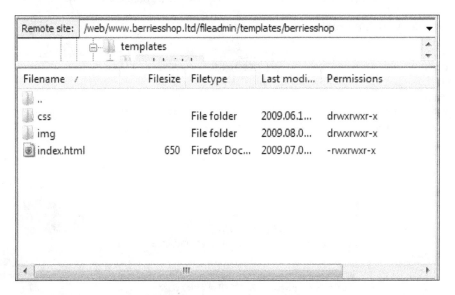

Upload the index.html (HTML template) file, CSS, and graphics to your web space, and change permissions on the file to 0555 to have read and write access if you're using a Unix system.

TypoScript setup and configuration

TypoScript is the scripting language that is used to tell TYPO3 how to create the web pages and is composed of two types of information as we mentioned before: constants and setup code.

Usually, the constants field is filled with extension configuration or values for repeatable use and setup—with the main setup to parse the HTML template.

To start editing TypoScript you need to create a page that will store the template TypoScript configuration. Usually, it is the parent page in the site tree. So let's create one:

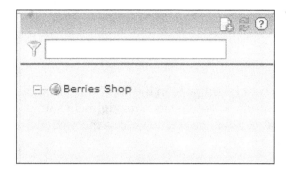

Click on the **+** icon and choose the position of the newly created page:

1. Untick the field **Hide page** and tick **Hide in menu** so that the page will not be displayed in the main menu, and designate a name by entering a Page title.

2. Save and close the document. If needed, reload the page tree by clicking on the reload icon below the site tree to see the created page.

3. Click on the **Template** button in the backend left menu, click on our new page **Home,** and hit the **Create template for a new site** button.

Now, when you have completed these steps you will have access to an already created template with the **HELLO WORLD!** example:

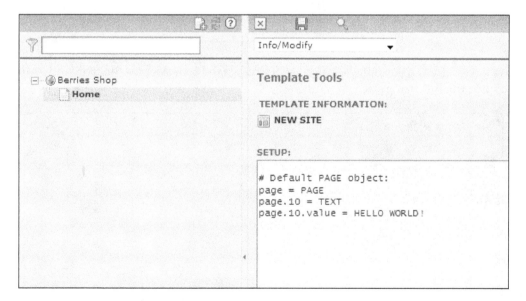

```
# Default PAGE object:
page = PAGE
page.10 = TEXT
page.10.value = HELLO WORLD!
```

Now you can oversee the chosen page in the TYPO3 backend. For page view, choose your created template and click on the icon (or right-click on page item). The context menu will be open and you will be able to choose the section **Show**, as seen in the following screenshot:

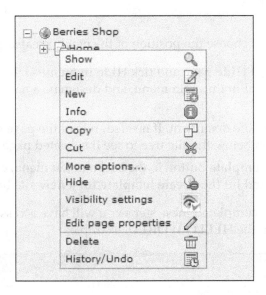

And if the added information was correct, the parsed template on the frontend will look like the following:

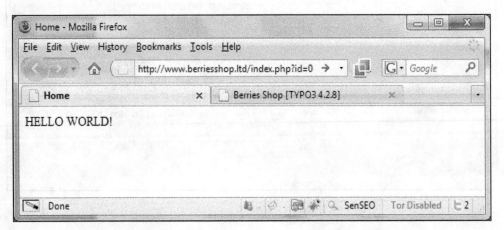

For a better understanding of what you are dealing with, you can edit the text like this so that you will have the text and image object:

```
# Default PAGE object:
page = PAGE
# Edit the text
page.10 = TEXT
page.10.value = This is TypoScript written by me!
# And add an image from our template folder:
page.20 = IMAGE
page.20.file = fileadmin/templates/berriesshop/logo.jpg
```

These are content objects: **cObjects**. You can use cObjects in your template such as the following:

- TEXT—to insert plain text or to output text from marked fields:

```
10 = TEXT
10.value = I wrote this text
10.lang.de = Ich schrieb diesen Text
```

- IMAGE—to insert images:

```
15 = IMAGE
15.file = fileadmin/img/logo.gif
15.stdWrap.typolink.parameter = 1 ## Wrap typolink and pointed
to page with uid 1
15.alttext = Your slogan title
```

- FILE — to insert a file; for example, to insert the HTML file for our webshop template:

```
page.10 = FILE
page.10.file = fileadmin/templates/berriesshop/index.html
```

- HMENU — to insert a hierarchical menu

- TMENU — to insert a text menu

- And others that you can find in the TSRef section of the TYPO3 documentation: http://typo3.org/documentation/document-library/references/doc_core_tsref/current

Inserting a template using TypoScript

We just created our own template and placed the markers. So, the next important step is to add that content from the TYPO3 backend.

You need to choose the section **Template**, and in the site tree, choose the page where you created the template. Click on the pencil icon near the **Setup** to open and to edit the TypoScript and to add our template:

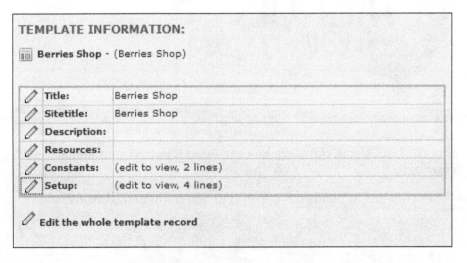

Here we will place the markers that we specified in the template. Let's insert the following code. First you have to start with the template configuration that specifies to TYPO3 what should be displayed in the code, and which charset and languages should be be used:

```
# LANGUAGE setup, here we enter the uID of language (default
# language has the value "0"), charset utf-8, the page
# language, and the html tag configuration
#-----------------------------------------------------------
config.linkVars = L
config.sys_language_uid = 0
config.metaCharset = utf-8
config.language = en
config.uniqueLinkVars = 1
config.htmlTag_setParams = xmlns="http://www.w3.org/1999/xhtml"
xml:lang="en" lang="en"
```

If you need a second language for your online shop, you can add a configuration for the alternative language page content. You can also add three or more languages using the [global] condition:

```
# CONFIG FOR 2ND LANGUAGE
#-----------------------------------------------------------
[globalVar = GP:L = 1]
config.sys_language_uid = 1
config.language = de
config.metaCharset = utf-8
plugin.meta.language = de
config.htmlTag_setParams = xmlns="http://www.w3.org/1999/xhtml"
xml:lang="de" lang="de"
[global]
# PAGE START
#-----------------------------------------------------------
   page = PAGE
   page {

# HEAD DATA - keywords and description
#-----------------------------------------------------------
   meta.keywords = shop, berries, berry
   meta.description = Our shop is the best!

# TEMPLATE - CSS and HTML file
#-----------------------------------------------------------
   stylesheet = fileadmin/templates/berriesshop/css/style.css
   10 = TEMPLATE
   10.template = FILE
   10.template.file = fileadmin/templates/berriesshop/index.html
   10.workOnSubpart = DOCUMENT_BODY
   10.marks {
```

Then you should add markers specifying enclosed resources—logos, content, and so on.

```
# LOGO - logo with link to "Home" page (that has ID=0) and
# alttext
#------------------------------------------------------------
   LOGO = IMAGE
   LOGO {
   file = fileadmin/templates/berriesshop/img/logo.jpg
   stdWrap.typolink.parameter = 0
   alttext = Berries Shop
   }
```

The next step is to add the top menu where the first level pages will be displayed. These pages will be specified in the sitemap:

```
# TOP MENU - this will be a text menu separated with "|"
# symbol (pipe)
#------------------------------------------------------------
   TOP-MENU= HMENU
   TOP-MENU{
   # the first level of TMENU (textmenu) items (1)
   1 = TMENU
   1.wrap =
     1 {
     noBlur = 1
### No state (NO): formatting for normal items
     NO{
        wrapItemAndSub = <span>|</span>
        allWrap = ||*| &#124; |*|
     }
### Current item (CUR)
     CUR = 1
     CUR{
        wrapItemAndSub = <span class="active">|</span>
        allWrap = ||*| &#124; |*|
     }
### Active state of item (ACT)
     ACT = 1
     ACT{
        wrapItemAndSub = <span class="active">|</span>
        allWrap = ||*| &#124; |*|
     }
   }
   }
```

Finally, you can add TypoScript to the main function—read the content data:

```
# LEFT MARKER - will be used for content and need to read the
# content data from BE LEFT column
#-----------------------------------------------------------
   LEFT = CONTENT
   LEFT {
      table = tt_content
      select.orderBy = sorting
      select.where = colPos = 1
   }

# CONTENT MARKER - will be used for content and need to read
# the content data from BE CENTER column
#-----------------------------------------------------------
   CONTENT = CONTENT
   CONTENT {
      table = tt_content
      select.orderBy = sorting
      select.where = colPos = 0
   }
```

You can specify configuration for the language menu. If your web space contains only one language, you can skip the following part of the code. If it contains several languages, you have to specify the extra language IDs in the line. For example:

```
LANGMENU.special.value = 0,1,2,5
# and extra values for displayed text
10.text = EN || DE || FR || RU

# LANGMENU - Graphical language menu with two languages -
# English and German. To use this function - you must upload
# a true type font file (*.ttf) on your webspace
# You could upload the font in the same way like template/css/image
files - using ssh, FTP software or from TYPO3 BE through "Filelist"
module on the left menu.

#-----------------------------------------------------------
LANGMENU = HMENU
LANGMENU.special = language
LANGMENU.special.value = 0,1
LANGMENU.1 = GMENU
LANGMENU.1 {
   NO {
```

```
      1 = IMAGE
      XY = 30,25
      format = gif
      backColor = #222222
      transparentColor = #222222
      10 = TEXT
      10.fontFile = fileadmin/fonts/verdana.ttf
      10.text = EN || DE
      10.fontSize = 14
      10.fontColor = #FFFFFF
      10.offset = 0,17
      10.niceText = 1
      10.align = center
    }
   ACT = 1
   ACT {
      1 = IMAGE
      XY = 30,25
      format = gif
      backColor = #222222
      transparentColor = #222222
      10 = TEXT
      10.fontFile = fileadmin/fonts/verdana.ttf
      10.text = EN || DE
      10.fontSize = 14
      10.fontColor = #FFFFFF
      10.offset = 0,17
      10.niceText = 1
      10.align = center
    }
  }
```

The footer information follows, which provides extra information to visitors about this page, the company, and so on:

```
# FOOTER MARKER - your copyright, contacts, etc.
#--------------------------------------------------------------
   FOOTER = TEXT
   FOOTER {
   value = All rights reserved, 2009 &copy;. www.berriesshop.ltd
   }
 }
```

After you add data, save it and close the setup.

Template Tools

TEMPLATE INFORMATION:

☷ **NEW SITE**

✎	Title:	NEW SITE
✎	Sitetitle:	
✎	Description:	
✎	Resources:	
✎	Constants:	(edit to view, 0 lines)
✎	Setup:	(edit to view, 153 lines)

Click here to edit whole template record

By clicking on the pencil icon, according to the title, enter the following information:

- **Title** — name of the template.
- **Sitetitle** — name of the web page. This value will be seen in the web page source as the `<title>` tag.
- **Description** — description of the website.

Many extensions (like the e-Commerce extension) come with additional configuration templates that are used to set up the configuration and style specific to the extension. These are called static templates. You add them to your TYPO3 by clicking on **Click here to edit whole template**, then clicking on the **Includes** tab, and adding the **CSS Styled Content (css_styled_content) template**. If this static template is not added, none the text that you insert in the TYPO3 backend (admin side) will be displayed.

Also, you need to add extension templates in this section, because for this template you have to use static templates too. You can find detailed information about it in the appropriate extension installation guide. You can find all the extension documentation in the TYPO3 repository — `http://typo3.org/extensions/repository/`.

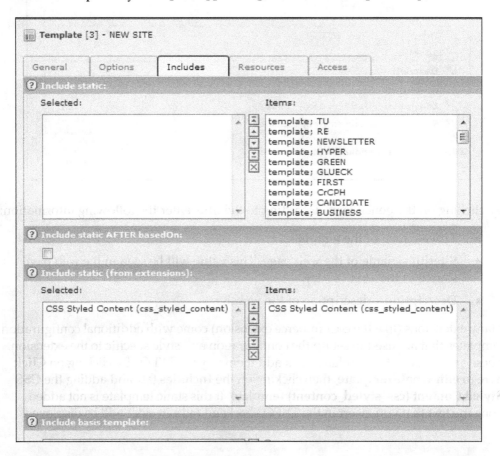

Save the added data and close the template.

Go to the template section **Constants** and add the following code. Using this code, we can specify the same fixed values:

- Maximum image width 520 px — image width can't be more than this value. This is useful for the correct page overview because large images can damage the look of the page.

- Replace sign @ with value "(at)" and encoding e-mail address with JavaScript. Replacing @ and encoding is useful to protect e-mails from spambots. Most of them collect e-mail addresses from the page HTML source.

```
# imgtext width - maximum image width is 520
# pixels
   styles.content.imgtext.maxW = 520
   styles.content.imgtext.linkWrap.width = 520

# spam protection - will replace the "@" symbol with (at).
# Works only, if the mailto link is set.
   config.spamProtectEmailAddresses = 2
   config.spamProtectEmailAddresses_atSubst = (at)
```

Save the added values and close the template.

You will need to edit this field again when working with new extensions that you will use. Mostly, there are stored settings for extensions in this area.

Finally, you should make sure that the template entry in **Clear** is checked for **Constants** and **Setup**. Also, make sure that **Rootlevel** is checked as well. You should mark these options (**Clear: Constants**, **Setup**, and **Rootlevel**) because page template needs to specify the correct rootline so that TYPO3 doesn't need to search the nearest template by tree level, which could be close to the beginning of the page tree.

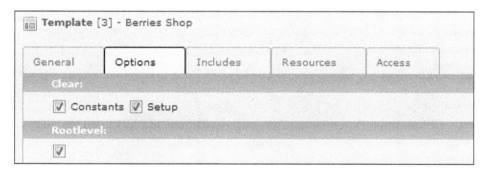

Adding and testing content

We added the template and entered the TypoScript configuration. We have to insert new pages for the correct work test now.

TYPO3 has great functions for creating several pages at the same time. Choose the section **Functions** from the left menu for creating new pages. You will see a page template in this section. You need to add page titles and click on **Create pages**.

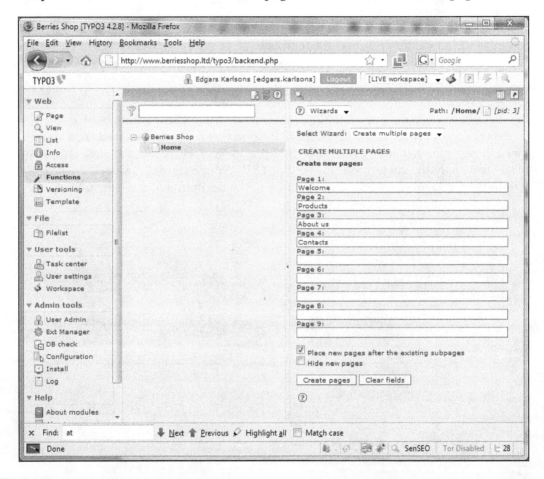

In the page created previously in our example, we only stored root template information. If we don't want that to be shown to the web page visitors, we need to do the following: click on the created page **Home** icon. Then, from the menu choose **Edit Page Settings**.

You can now edit the page setting. You need to change the page setting to **Shortcut**. On the **General** tab of the page settings, you can set the page type to **Shortcut**. The page will refresh and there will now be a **Shortcut** tab. On this tab, you specify the page to which this page should be linked.

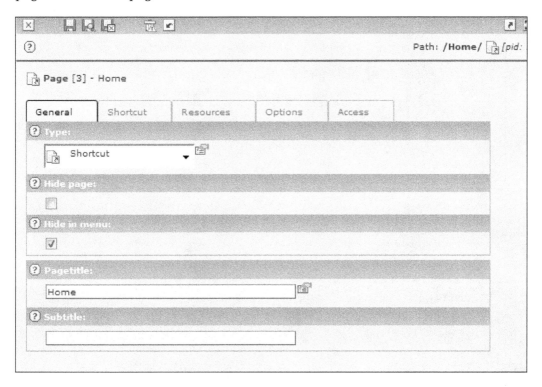

Choose one of the pages in the **Page** section. Add some text and image for the result test. You can add text and image by clicking on the **+** icon on the **Page** module in the necessary column. Also, you can use the button **Create page content,** as seen in the following screenshot:

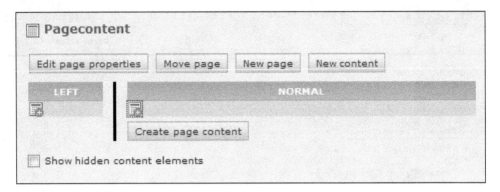

For example, you could choose the content element **Text** or **Text with image**:

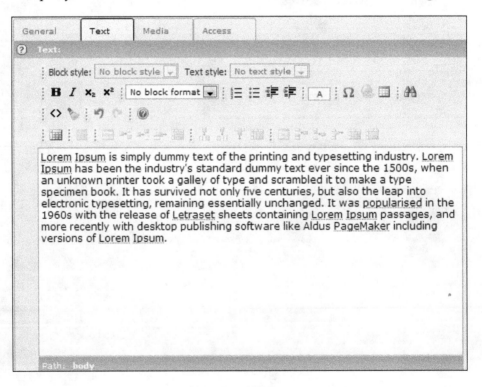

Entry fields (TCA fields) are divided into four parts:

- **General** — base information about records: title, subtitle, links, data, author, among others.

- **Text** — RTE (Rich Text Editor) part where you can add text, like in common office software text editors.

- **Media** — for adding images: size, links, title, and alt text tag values, position, number of columns, and so on.

- **Access** — access to record. You can set here that the record will only be seen by FE (frontend) users who are authorized or just the opposite, that is, after authorization, the record is hidden. You can use FE user groups if they exist.

Save the record and view it from the website FE.

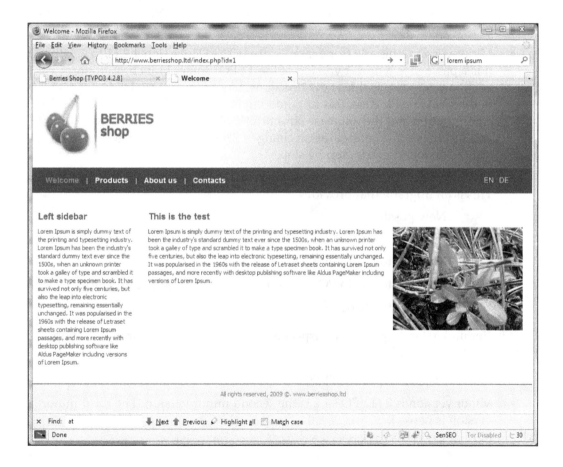

Upgrading TYPO3 to a newer version

Almost all programs become more and more functional with newer versions. It's the same with TYPO3. If you upgrade your programs to their newest version, you can use the new functions and there are more possibilities. Thanks to the co-operation of the TYPO3 users and the team working on this CMS, TYPO3 has become very secure. For updating TYPO3, it is important that your website has the latest system functionality and safety.

We can divide TYPO3 upgrading into three parts:

- Patch version upgrade (for example, from version 4.2.11 to 4.2.12): This upgrade should be made to avoid bugs and to implement repairs of bugs. Relative patch version upgrade is easy to manage. For the most part, it can be done with just the TYPO3 source patch—replacing this with the patch files on the web server. You can find the patch on the TYPO3 download site: `http://typo3.org/download/packages/`

- Minor version upgrade (for example, from TYPO3 version 4.2.11 to 4.3.0): It is a passage to a newer version of the TYPO3 lower branch. A minor version upgrade provides new functions, bug fixes, and probably changes in the TYPO3 API. Also, this upgrade might provide changes to the TYPO3 configuration and the database structure. This upgrade is more complicated and includes some configuration changes. Therefore, we will go through the minor version upgrade step by step.

- Major version upgrade (for example, from TYPO3 version 4.3.1 to 5.0): This is an upgrade that provides:
  - New possibilities
  - Bug fixes
  - Changes to the coding API/architecture
  - Changes to the TYPO3 configuration (including TypoScript)
  - Changes to the database

For a better understanding, we can inspect the current version of our online shop that is TYPO3 version 4.2.11:

- Major version is 4 (fourth TYPO3 major version).
- Minor version is 2 (TYPO3 4.x is the second minor version. The third minor version is newer).
- Patch version is 11 (TYPO3 4.2 version eleventh patch upgrade by turns).

TYPO3 is extended into two different packages:

- Source package— this contains TYPO3 base code named "TYPO3 core". If you upgrade TYPO3 to a newer version, you will use this kind of a package.

- Dummy package— this contains folders of file structure like **fileadmin** (where all your added files and templates are downloaded by default—and this folder you can manage through the **Filelist** module), **typo3conf** (where the TYPO3 configuration is stored—the file `localconf.php`, configuration cache, and TYPO3 local extensions), and so on. We can say that these folders contain data that in the course of time are saved or are stocked up, adding new content—for example images, templates, configuration setups, and extensions. If you upgrade TYPO3 to a newer version, you shouldn't upgrade the dummy package, as you could lose important data.

TYPO3 minor version update

First of all, if you upgrade your TYPO3 old version and update it, for example from 4.1.x to TYPO3 4.3.x, you should remember that it is a large change over the whole minor version. In each version there are changes in the database. Therefore, updating TYPO3 from 4.1.x to 4.3.x can cause errors and you will have to manage changes manually. The TYPO3 core team is working on the newer versions to be compatible with the previous version. So it is recommended that you upgrade from the 4.1.x version of your TYPO3 to 4.2.x and then to the newer 4.3.x version.

To upgrade TYPO3, you will need a newer TYPO3 source package that you can download from the TYPO3 web page: `http://typo3.org/download/packages/`.

You have to unpack this source package and replace the old source content with the new one. If you use Unix systems, choose `*.tar` packages and unpack them with the command:

```
tar xzf typo3_src-4.3.1.tar.gz
```

Create a symbolic link. If you use Unix or a similar operational system, create the symbolic link name `typo3_src`:

```
ln -s /var/www/typo3_src-4.3.1 /var/www/example.com/typo3_src
```

If you use Windows 7 or Windows Vista, in the Command Prompt program (CMD.exe) create the following junction:

```
mklink /D C:\xampp\htdocs\berriesshop\typo3_src-4.3.1 C:\xampp\
htdocs\berriesshop\typo3_src
```

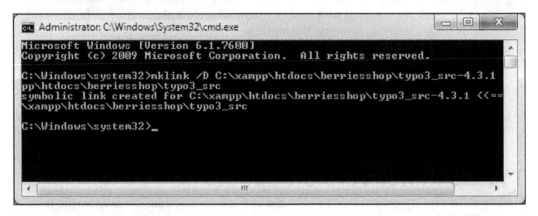

The source folder stores content that will replace the old source package:

- misc
- t3lib
- typo3
- index.php

After you upgrade the source package, go on to the TYPO3 Install Tool. The easiest way is to use the TYPO3 backend—choosing **Install** from the left menu section. Maybe **ENABLE_INSTALL_TOOL** is deleted for security reasons or the file has become outdated (**ENABLE_INSTALL_TOOL** file is available for one hour after its creation). If so, then go on to the section **User Settings** and choose the tab **Admin functions**. In this section, you can create the **ENABLE_INSTALL_TOOL** file (there's no need to use FTP).

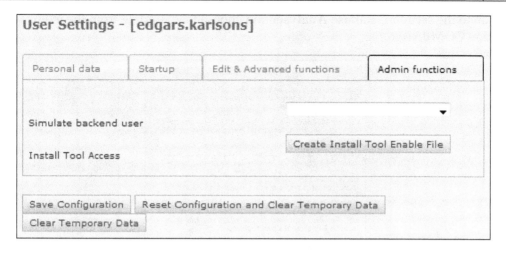

TYPO3 update

Using the TYPO3 Install tool (`http://www.example.com/typo3/install/` or selecting it from backend menu section **Install**), choose **Update Wizard**. You can set up new extensions in this section that are available from TYPO3 version 4.3 if necessary. For example:

- recycler: This extension deletes tables that are marked as deleted or un-deletes them. This is a useful extension because there can be situations where some testing elements are needed (pages, contain) and these elements, after tests, are marked with "delete" but aren't physically deleted. These "deleted" elements are unnecessarily stored. Using this extension, you can dispose of these tables fully. But remember to use this extension carefully because you will not be able to restore this data.

- t3editor: This is a TypoScript's editor with syntax highlighting and code completion for TypoScript. Using this extension, you can oversee TypoScript easier and you can manage TypoScript faster. If you type some code, the extension will offer to end the entered TypoScript function.

- scheduler: This is a cron-like task planner. You can use this extension to complete tasks in time. With this extension, you can complete the test task at the moment.

Go on to the section **Database Analyser** and choose table update from the menu section **COMPARE**:

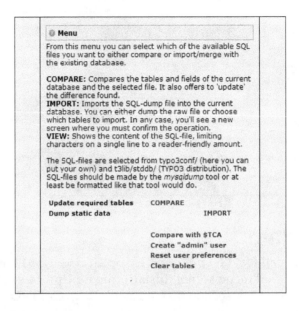

You will see the changes that have to be done. If you don't make these changes, TYPO3 will operate with errors. We did the test and the results are: errors were for TYPO3 installations that contained definitions for more than one language. Approve the changes and check. A repeat test will be required if the old tables get deleted. Also, these tables were in use for some installed and after-deleted extensions. We recommend going through all the stages in this section.

⚠ Table and field definitions should be updated

There seems to be a number of differences between the database and the selected SQL-file. Please execute in order to update your database:

Add fields

☑ **select/deselect all**

☑ ALTER TABLE be_groups ADD fileoper_perms tinyint(4) NOT NULL default '0';

☑ ALTER TABLE sys_lockedrecords ADD feuserid int(11) unsigned NOT NULL default '0';

☑ ALTER TABLE pages_language_overlay ADD doktype tinyint(3) unsigned NOT NULL default '0';

☑ ALTER TABLE pages_language_overlay ADD url varchar(255) NOT NULL default '';

☑ ALTER TABLE pages_language_overlay ADD urltype tinyint(4) unsigned NOT NULL default '0';

After the database checkup, we recommend checking and updating the database Reference Index in the backend left menu by choosing the section **DB Check** and from the drop-down menu choosing **Manage Reference Index**. Clear all caches and check the web page view in the frontend.

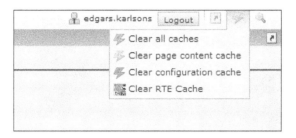

Summary

Templates are used for adding design in TYPO3 like in all web pages and content management systems. You don't have to know PHP for adding templates to TYPO3. Usually, you can set up templates in the same way as for statistical HTML web pages. It is necessary to remember that in TYPO3 there is a difference between the two types of templates — TypoScript configuration templates and HTML layout templates.

TypoScript configuration at the TYPO3 backend is stored in two separate fields — setup and constants. You can use cObjects in your template. TYPO3 has great functions for creating several pages at the same time.

In the next chapter, we will describe TYPO3 e-Commerce plugins you can use to provide payment possibility in your online shop. Also, we will describe the most popular payments, such as online and offline payments using a card and the PayPal system, which is the most popular form of payment at the moment.

3
Singularity of TYPO3 E-Commerce Plugins

In the first chapter, we saw how to install TYPO3 and choose the appropriate extension. And in the second chapter, we explained how to configure the designed template and discussed the most frequently encountered issues. Now we can move onto adding the e-Commerce plugins to the online shop.

This chapter explains how to add the e-Commerce plugins to the online shop that is based on TYPO3. The topics covered are:

- Payment add-ins
- Upgrading to a newer version

By the end of this chapter you should have completed the e-Commerce plugin adding process for the chosen shop options.

TYPO3 E-Commerce plugins

TYPO3 e-Commerce plugins provide a payment facility for your online shop. It is possible to use quite a few extensions for TYPO3 at the moment. You need to choose the extension that is suitable for your online shop: one that suits the shop's requirements and extension options.

There are two extensions from TYPO3 TER (TYPO3 Extension Repository) that are popular and typical:

- Shop System (tt_products) by Franz Holzinger: This is the most used (the extension that has the maximum number of downloads in the TYPO3 repository) e-Commerce extension. This extension provides product management, product articles, PayPal/card/bank transfer payments, special offers, product variants, voucher system, and so on.

- Webformat Shop System (extendedshop) by Mauro Lorenzutti: This is a fast-growing extension that provides functions such as product management, color/size variants, order management, VAT management, orders tracking, products categories, multilingual product entries, and so on.

- Commerce (commerce) by Ingo Schmitt, Volker Graubaum, and Thomas Hempel: This is a comparatively new e-Commerce extension (it's in the Beta stage now, which means it will improve further). This extension provides most of the functions that you need for an online shop. Like the other two extensions, *commerce* provides functions such as product/categories management, stock management, product variants – sizes/colors, VAT management, scaled price groups for orders, and so on.

We can say that the Webformat Shop System by Mauro Lorenzutti is probably more teachable and easier to set up. But Shop System by Franz Holzinger has more functions. If you can financially back the development of the Shop System, you can get access to the newer versions of this extension that support new functions. The Shop System extension that we used from TER, at the time of writing this book, does not support multilingual templates. If you need to use an extension for multilingual content in your websites and you have multiple languages, you can translate templates and add the translated template in the TypoScript configuration using the condition [global]. For example, you can add this line in the code:

```
plugin.tt_products.templateFile = fileadmin/templates/specialcards/
template.html
```

Add this line into the template:

```
config.linkVars = L
...
config.sys_language_uid = 0
plugin.tt_products.templateFile = fileadmin/templates/berriesshop/
shop_english.html
...
```

And specify the template for an alternative language:

```
[globalVar = GP:L = 1]
...
config.sys_language_uid = 1
plugin.tt_products.templateFile = fileadmin/templates/berriesshop/
shop_german.html
...
[global]
```

You should remember that the `path` (target) for the template location is the same as the main template location.

 When you update extensions to the newest versions, files will be modified and none of the changes that were in the extension folder will be saved. Therefore, you can lose the translated template and the configured design of the template, which wastes a lot of time and work. We recommend locating a template outside of the folder of extension installation.

There are several twists and turns for every extension. It is useful to read manuals before you choose and set up an e-Commerce extension.

Payment add-ins

Credit cards and debit cards with overdraft and credit limits are the most popular and handy way to pay for goods on the Internet. If you use this kind of payment in your website, you should add the specified codes for information input and sending. These requirements are from financial companies and banks for transactions security. It can be tough.

Payment systems can be unitary by one company that provide card payments in that country or some region. Also, banks can provide their services for credit and debit card payments.

The most popular means of payment are:

- Cash
- Transfers
- Online payments using card
- Offline payments using card
- PayPal and similar payment systems (intermediary services for payment by transfer (they are the most popular form of payments)
- Payment using SMS through the phone

If you decide to support card payments on your website, you might have to invest extra money—connecting this service, purchase costs for SSL security certificate, and monthly costs for system support from the bank. SSL is a compulsory requirement for credit/debit card processing. These service payment procedures vary according to the banks and their pricelists.

On average, an SSL certificate can cost anywhere from a few hundred to a few thousand US dollars. It depends on the security level and the certification authority identification. The most important aspects of using an SSL certificate are how these certificates will be identified on different Internet browsers and which certificate authority (CA) they have. Popular and well-known companies in this area are VeriSign and Thawte.

The PayPal payment system is one of the most popular ones for goods in TYPO3-based online shops that use e-Commerce extensions. Shop System, Webformat Shop System, and Commerce all support using PayPal.

Setting up a PayPal test account

A secure way to test PayPal is to set up a PayPal test account. You can create a test account by visiting this web page:

```
https://developer.paypal.com/
```

PayPal offers two kinds of merchant accounts:

- PayPal merchant account:
  - ○ Without a monthly payment
  - ○ With a commission of 2.9% to 1.9% + $0.30 per transaction

- PayPal Pro merchant account:
  - ○ With a monthly payment of $30
  - ○ With a commission of 2.9% to 2.2% + $0.30 per transaction

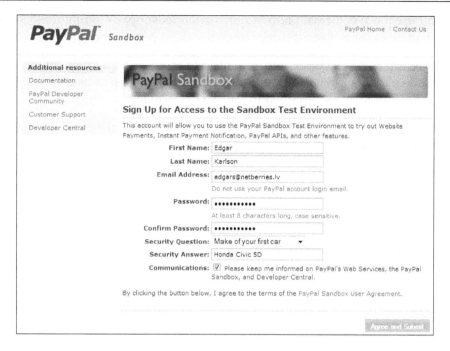

After registration, you can create the test account for the seller and buyer.

If we are going to use the PayPal service together with the Shop System (tt_products) extension, we need two extra extensions that we can find in the TYPO3 TER:

- Payment code library (paymentlib)
- Paypal Payment Suite (paymentlib_paypal)

When you use the Webformat Shop System (extendedshop) e-Commerce extension, you need an extra extension for the former for Paypal (wss_paypal).

For the extension's correct operation, you need to input some settings (identification of the seller—e-mail, path URL to PayPal, return URL to your website, and header image for PayPal) that are described in the extension manual.

Go to the Extension Manager, choose extension, and click on the extension title **paymentlib_paypal**.

A detailed overview of the extension will open. From the top drop-down menu, you can choose **Settings** and add the necessary information.

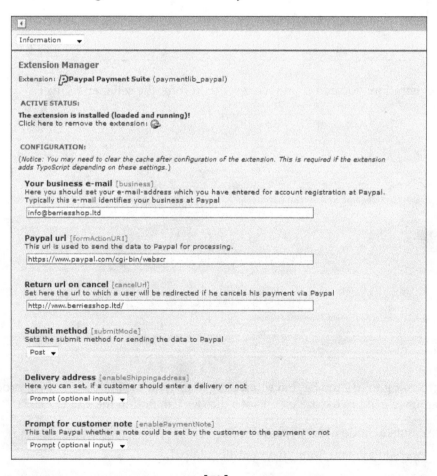

Upgrading to a newer version

Common extensions like the e-Commerce extensions are updated quite frequently. We recommend that you check, the version of the extension that is in use in your website at TYPO3 TER; you can verify which versions are available.

You can check extensions and the available versions in the **Ext Manager**. Choose **Import extensions** from the top menu and click on the **Retrieve/Update** button.

After the data update, you should choose **Check for extension updates** from the top menu. You will see a list of extensions that has the newest versions. If there are no newer versions of the extensions, this list will be empty.

Check for extension updates ▾

Extension Manager

Display shy extensions: ☑

THERE ARE NEW VERSIONS OF THE FOLLOWING EXTENSIONS IN THE TER

Extension Ext-Key Local Remote Location Upload-Comment

☑ Include not loaded extensions into listing
☑ Display the list of changed files

VERSION INFORMATION

Last update of list of extensions: 2009-09-15 05:07
Use "Retrieve/Update" in "Import Extensions" section to get/update the list.

You can check for the extension update manually too, using the TYPO3 TER website:

http://www.typo3.org/repository/

You can type the title of the extension that you want to check for updates and compare it with the version that is in use. If a newer version is found, and it is compatible with the TYPO3 version and PHP version on the server side, you can download it. In the **Ext manager**, you should choose **Import extensions** from the top menu and choose **Overwrite any existing extension**.

Import extensions ▼

Extension Manager

Group by: Category ▼ Show: Details ▼
Show obsolete: ☑

EXTENSIONS IN TYPO3 EXTENSION REPOSITORY

⑦

List or look up reviewed extensions

[   ] | Look up |

Connect to the current mirror and retrieve the current list of available plugins from the TYPO3 Extension Reposit
| Retrieve/Update | (last update: 15-09-09 05:07)

Found a security problem? Please get in touch with us!
If you think you have found a security issue in TYPO3 or an extension, please contact the TYPO3 security team!

PRIVACY NOTICE:
When you interact with the online repository, server information may be sent and stored in the repository for sta

UPLOAD EXTENSION FILE DIRECTLY (.T3X):

Upload extension file (.t3x):

C:\Users\Desktop\paymentlib_0.3.2.t3x | Browse... |
... to location:
Local (../typo3conf/ext/) ▼
☑ Overwrite any existing extension!
| Upload extension file |

Summary

TYPO3 e-Commerce plugins provide a payment facility in your online shop. There are two extensions from the TYPO3 Extension Repository that are more popular and typical—Shop System and Webformat Shop System. There are several twists and turns for every extension. It is useful to read manuals before you choose and set up an e-Commerce extension. The PayPal payment system is the most popular way to pay for goods in TYPO3-based online shops that use e-Commerce extensions.

If extensions are in use for a long time, they become outdated and don't support some functions. So, it is useful to check for extension updates.

In the next chapter we will describe setting up online shop requirements, explaining how to set up a catalogue of products, how to prepare product-descriptive information (images and textual information), and how to organize the structure of the catalogue.

4
Catalogue—Setting Up Online Shop Requirements

This chapter describes how to prepare information for publishing in your online shop created with TYPO3. Information can be images, text, and an item's categorization by size, color, products' campaigns, and so on.

Framework and content

In general, if you are running e-Commerce information you often need to summarize from different sources, and the information preparation format can be very different. We recommend storing information in CSV (Comma Separated Values) files where you can:

- Categorize information and store information like tables. This method of storing information provides easy viewing and may require sorting information in software like Microsoft Excel or Open Office Calc.

- Avoid text formatting. You don't need to remove the formatting for stored information using the RTE—Rich Text Editor—in TYPO3, which is similar to most of the available WYSIWYG editors.

If you are storing information in CSV files, information takes less space, is mobile, and is easy to distribute. CSV files provide accessibility on most of the computer platforms: Windows, Mac OS, and Linux systems.

If you configured your web page so that all the images through the GIFBUILDER are generated like jpeg files, we recommend adding images in the PNG format. Some general benefits of this format are:

- High image quality
- Smaller size

The easiest way to work with the CSV data format is to use a third-party extension, for example, **wil_importcsv**. You should note that this extension is in the Alpha state. This means that the extension is in the early stage of development. If you want to use that kind of extension, we recommend backing up the database in case of errors.

For using this extension, utilize the Extension manager module and download the extension to your TYPO3 installation. If the installation is successful you'll be able to choose the new backend module **Import CSV**, as seen in the following screenshot:

After the installation, this extension supports access to database tables and tt_content, but you should set up an extra configuration to provide extension supports to other tables—for example, tt_products.

Go to the module **Page** and choose the first-level page from sitemap. In our example, this is the first-level page where page templates are stored. You should configure some of the options. Choose the section **Options** and add this line of code, as shown in the following screenshot:

```
mod.web_txwilimportcsvM1.tables = ALL
```

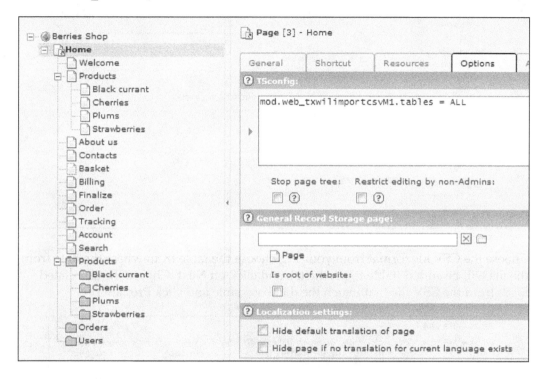

In this way you provide full access to all the tables for users who have administrator rights. If you want to use the extension **wil_importcsv** for some definite tables, separate the tables' names with commas:

```
mod.web_txwilimportcsvM1.tables = tt_products, tt_products_articles,
tx_myextension
```

Save the entered TypoScript configuration and go to the backend module **Import CSV** as shown in the following screenshot:

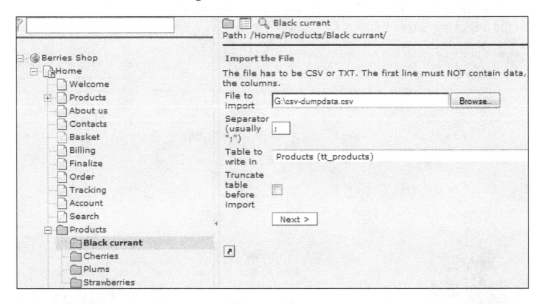

Choose the CSV file format from your PC, choose the table from where the data from the file will be added (table tt_products), and click on **Next**. Choose the associated fields from the CSV file that match the database table and click **Preview**:

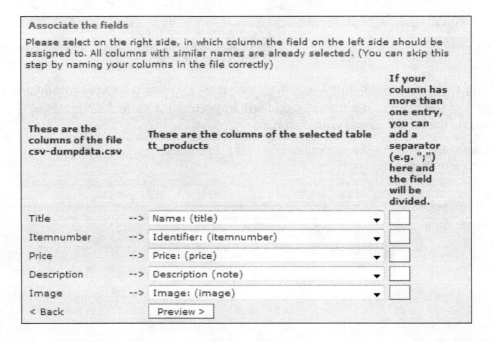

You can see a CSV file in the following screenshot. This file will be imported to the tt_products table. Remember that the first line should contain column names (not product data). You will use column names for CSV fields mapping:

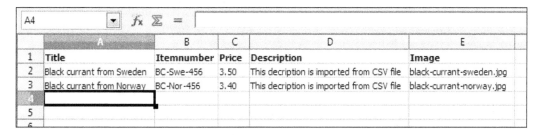

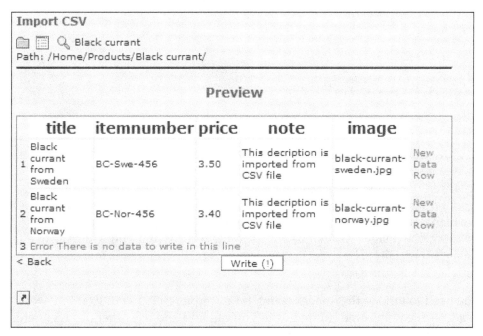

If all the marked fields are marked correctly, click on **Write (!)**. Then, data from the CSV file will be added to the web page database.

New data will be seen in the frontend and backend sections if the CSV field mappings are successful, as you can see in the following screenshot:

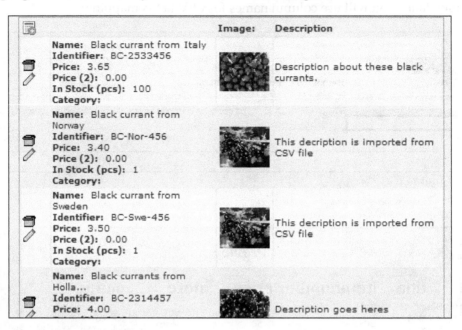

Images aren't stored in the database—there are stored references to the corresponding folders where images are uploaded instead. You should specify image filenames in the CSV dump file (not file embedding). If you use file embedding, the images will not be added to the records and you will have to attach the images manually. The extension tt_products by default reads images from the folder: /uploads/pics/.

So you need to upload the images using, for example, FTP. In our example we used a CSV file with some columns, but you can add and use other product fields: www, subtitle, inStock, and so on.

Adding products to the online shop

For adding a new product to the online shop, you need to first prepare:

- Accordant configuration for plugins (in our shop, it is tt_products). Also, you need to add plugins into the web shop.
- Sysfolder—where you will store product records.
- Created category and product records.

In our example we created records dividing each page like a separate category; categories read information from a separate sysfolder. The easiest way to do this dividing is to create a new folder in the site map where child folders will be stored, as in the following screenshot:

For creating a SysFolder, from the page module you need to click on the New page icon in the root page. SysFolder creation is similar to new page creation. You need to choose **SysFolder** in the drop-down menu, as you can see in the following screenshot:

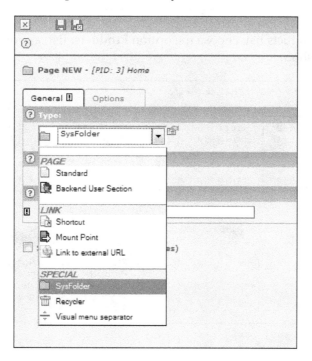

Working with TYPO3, you will rarely be in a situation where you need to create special system folders. You can also store records for specific extensions on regular pages ("Standard" type). By adding several parts, your web page might grow to the point where it will be difficult to find the required page where records are stored (for example, for editing these records)..

Next you need to create pages for product categories. In these pages, the online shop extension will be included by adding the new content element **Shop System** and adding this element in the column that you are using for placing the main content.

First we choose the just created page **Black currant** from the example and add in this page the new content element **Shop System**, as you can see in the following screenshot:

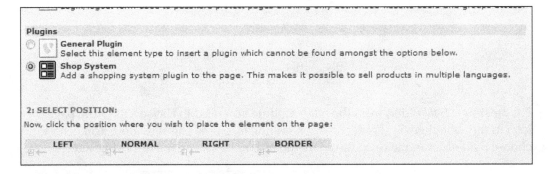

For adding the products list, choose the option **Products: list**, as you can see in the following screenshot:

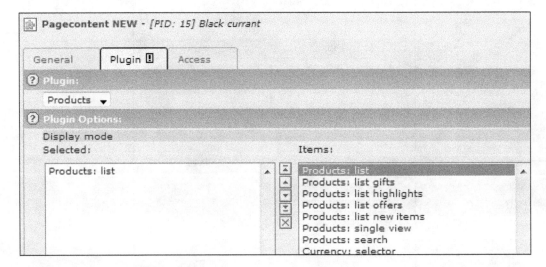

Choose the system folder from where the created records will be read. If you have selected to view the list of black currants that will be sold, choose the sysfolder **Black currant,** as shown in the following screenshot:

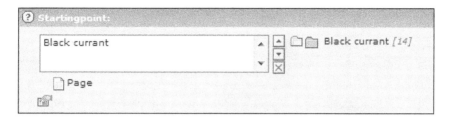

Save the page and add options for other sections in the same way. We choose SysFolder for the first level page. To set up this option, below the section **Startingpoint** choose the extra option **Infinite,** (as shown in the following screenshot), which means data is being read from the SysFolder. This means that all data will be placed in TYPO3 frontend, independent of subfolder quantity.

Creating product records

You need to create product records for displaying products in the online shop pages. These records will contain the product description, the name of the product, property, and the image of the product.

So now you need to create a new product record in the child SysFolder, Black currant. Create a new record and add the necessary information, as you can see in the following screenshot:

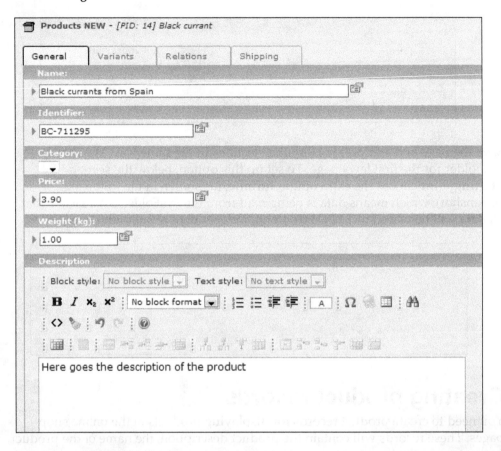

You can fill in the following:

- **Name** – name of the product

- **Identifier** – if you have a large number of products or you need to follow up the product with a waybill

- **Category** – we are using only pages instead of categories

- **Price** – currency will be configured separately, so you don't need to input a currency type like USD or EUR.

- **Weight** – product weight; this can be for delivery cost calculations, for example

- **Image** – image of the product

Also, you can provide extra information about the product, such as various kinds of weight packing and various sizes (for example, you could display S, M, L, and XL sizes of one cloth model).

When you add all products pages, it will look like the following:

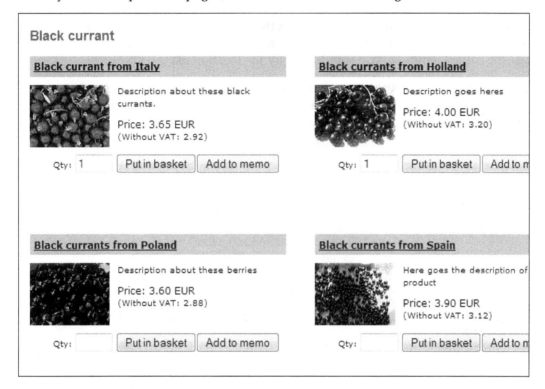

 We used the Banana shop template that is incorporated with the tt_ products extension and modified this template from a `<table>` tag-based template to a `<div>` tag template with two columns.

For creating your own template, you can choose some already prepared templates that can be found in the extension `tt_products` folder. Relative to the site root, the default templates are in the folder: `/typo3conf/ext/tt_products/template/`.

You should remember that the template is divided into subparts, for example:

- ###ITEM_LIST_TEMPLATE### is used to show the product list in the frontend. Also, this subpart is used for showing the search results.
- ###ITEM_SINGLE_DISPLAY### is used for product singleview.
- ###BASKET_TEMPLATE### is used to see the basket content.

These subparts are numerous, so for template configuration you should have a basic knowledge of xHTML/CSS and the visual xHTML modeling software. Also, you should know template development well. As an alternative, you can use the default template to manage the minimal required changes to configure the template for your web page.

If you use a default template, copy it from the `tt_products` template folder and add to the `/fileadmin/` folder where the base template of your web page is located. To use the copied template, you should specify the location using TypoScript.

Open the backend module, **Template**, choose the site root page where all the template configurations are stored, and manage changes by adding the field product template's relative location with respect to the root page in `Setup`. Also, add the template name:

```
plugin.tt_products.templateFile = fileadmin/templates/bs/products_
en.html
```

```
tt_products don't offer multilingual templates. So if you make
configuration for multilanguage page you should add options using
TypoScript like you did with language configuration:
```

```
config.linkVars = L
config.sys_language_uid = 0
[...]
config.language = en
plugin.tt_products.templateFile = fileadmin/templates/bs/products_
en.html
[globalVar = GP:L = 1]
config.sys_language_uid = 1
[...]
config.language = de
plugin.tt_products.templateFile = fileadmin/templates/bs/products_
de.html
[global]
```

Extra options

For the correct functioning of the online shop, you need to create extra pages:

- Page for billing (if needed)
- Page for basket/cart
- Page for shop admin (for the administrator needs of order processing)

We also added an extra option in the template Constants part:

```
### Image size (100px)
plugin.tt_products.maxW_listRoot = 100
plugin.tt_products.maxW_listHasChilds = 100
plugin.tt_products.maxW_list = 100
### pID (page ID) where is located the additional pages like basket,
payments
plugin.tt_products.PIDbasket = 19
plugin.tt_products.PIDstoreRoot = 8
plugin.tt_products.PIDdelivery = 21
plugin.tt_products.PIDpayment = 20
plugin.tt_products.PIDmemo = 22
plugin.tt_products.PIDbilling = 20
plugin.tt_products.PIDtracking = 23
plugin.tt_products.PIDfinalize = 24
```

You can install all of these options and others through the **Constants editor** of the template, as shown in the following screenshot:

If you specify page ID, make sure that the indicated page contains the necessary functions. If there is an error, the online shop will respond incorrectly to data input or not work at all.

For example, when we specify values in the template constants part:

```
plugin.tt_products.PIDbasket = 19
```

we need to add the plugin **Basket: content** to the page with ID 19 (as shown in the following screenshot):

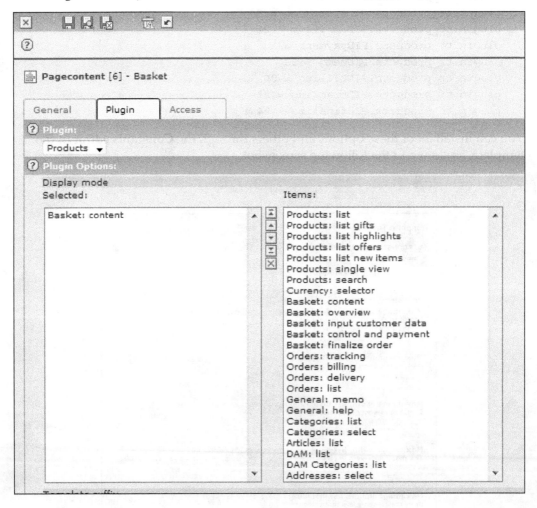

After using the examples described here, we recommend trying other functions that can be used with this extension. For example, can use functions like the following:

- Special price offers
- Campaign products/Special products
- Possibility to pay with discount vouchers

All the information about the extra functions of tt_products can be found in the extension specification in the TYPO3 repository.

Summary

If you are running an e-Commerce website, you often need to summarize from different sources, and the information preparation format can be very different. If you are storing information in CSV files, the information takes little space and is mobile and easy to distribute. CSV files provide accessibility on most of the computer platforms — Windows, MacOS, and Linux systems.

Categories read information from a separate SysFolder. Creating SysFolder is similar to creating a new page.

You need to create product records for displaying products in the online shop pages. These records will contain the product description, the name of the product, properties, and the image of the product.

In the next chapter we will describe the organization of unregistered and registered users, and how to add features for advanced user's options.

5
Shop Users—Profiles for Unregistered and Registered Users

This chapter covers the organization of unregistered and registered users, adding features for advanced user options, and also describes the shopping process scheme for users. The topics covered are:

- Profiles of the users
- History of the orders
- Buying basket information
- Confirmation by e-mail
- Discounts
- User groups

By the end of this chapter, you'll know all the user-managing options.

The importance of registering users

You might need the users' register every day for growing your business, promoting traffic, and improving finances.

For example, you might need to look for the favorite products depending on the different user groups. Using the users' register will reveal information about important data that will help improve your online shop.

Also, you can offer discounts and campaign products that are just for registered users who purchase something in your online shop repeatedly.

User registration

You can register users on your online shop in many ways:

- Using special extensions for registration (the user needs to fill out a registration form)
- When customers complete a transaction by buying a product in your online shop (the system can send access information—username and password— after purchasing, and the user can use this information to log in to the online shop like a registered user)

The most popular registration form for TYPO3 is the extension **sr_feuser_register** (Front End User Registration). You can see the **Users** folder in the site tree, as shown in the following screenshot:

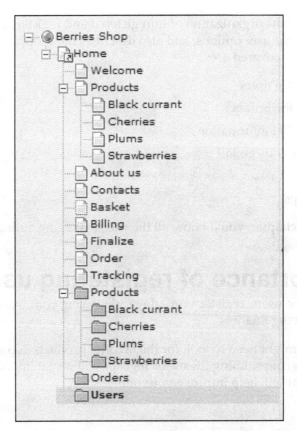

You can add the user registration extension by following these steps:

1. Download the extension from the TYPO3 repository.

2. Using the Extension Manager, install the extension.

3. Create a new SysFolder in your site tree (in this SysFolder, users and user groups will be saved together, if there are any).

4. Add the registration form and set up the required option into the page for user registry.

5. Add the template for the registry form (Old Style or CSS).

6. Continue further Typoscript configuration using the Constant Editor. It is important to know that extensions can usually be improved with new functions and therefore the configuration of TypoScript can change. You can find these changes in the updated extensions manual and the instructions in the TYPO3 repository at the accordant extension. You can read the instructions online or download them in the SXW format (open with OpenOffice if you are using Windows/Linux or with NeoOffice if you using MacOS) through the **Extension Manager**.

7. For extension installation, you should choose **Ext Manager** (Extension Manager) from the left menu section. This manager is a module of TYPO3 that provides management of the extensions' functions, such as import of new extensions, install/uninstall, and upgrading extensions to newer versions.

8. As a first step before you start the installation, choose **Settings** from the top drop-down menu. Check **Enable extensions without review** in the checkbox, as you can see in the following screenshot:

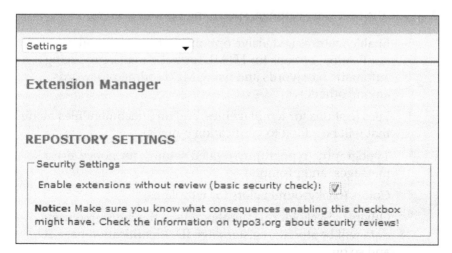

This check enables you to import extensions (and extensions without review) from the TYPO3 TER directly. We will discuss this further in Chapter 8.

Next, go to the section **Import extensions** (through the top drop-down menu) and check for newer extensions by downloading the list from the TYPO3 extension repository (click on **Retrieve/Update**). After the list is updated, type the extension name or keyword you are searching for and click on **Import**. The extension will be imported to your web space, or if the extension is already installed and there's a newer version, you will be able to update the extension:

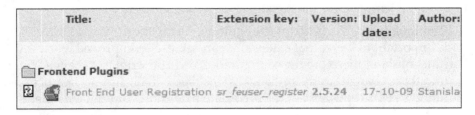

After the extension is set up, you should configure it using TypoScript. If the chosen extension has `fail` in the `constants.txt`, you can set up the template through the **Template** module. You can configure it now as follows:

1. Choose the module **Template** and the page from the sitemap where the template is saved.

2. From the module menu (top drop-down menu), choose **Contant Editor.** Then, from the **Category** section, choose the extension that you want to configure. In our example it will be **PLUGIN.TX_SRFEUSERREGISTER_Pi1** (note that this title is the title of the extension configuration syntax).

3. Manage the necessary settings, specifying options such as:

    ° Enable features (extensive options that include sending notification, options for HTML format e-mails, producing automatic passwords and using MD5 coding passwords, among others.)

    ° Files (options for template files, and an attachment files menu that will be added to verification e-mails)

    ° Typography (typography-related settings for notice, error messages, and prompts)

    ° Colors (background colors for templates)

    ° Others (a SysFolder ID number where the registered users' data will be stored: register page ID, identification page ID, and so on.)

4. After these changes, you should save the options by clicking on **Save document** at the top of the page.

For frontend users' registration extension, the addition of a static template is necessary. You can do this by following these steps:

From the top drop-down menu, choose the **Info/Modify** option. You can edit the template by clicking on **Edit the whole template record**. Through this section, all fields connected to the template can be edited.

Choose the table **Includes** and add the static template by clicking on its title in the **Items** column:

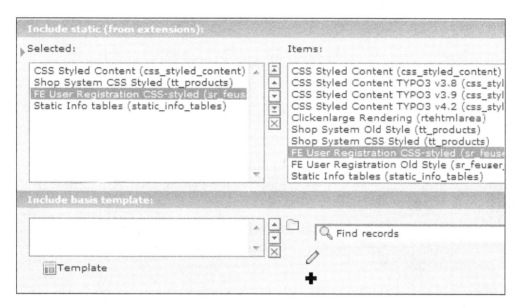

You should add the selected static template of the extension to the **Selected** column after the **CSS Styled Content** (css_styled_content) template. Otherwise, this template will not work, because css_styled_content is the base static template that is responsible for page layout and mapping.

Save the options and move on to adding extensions into the page.

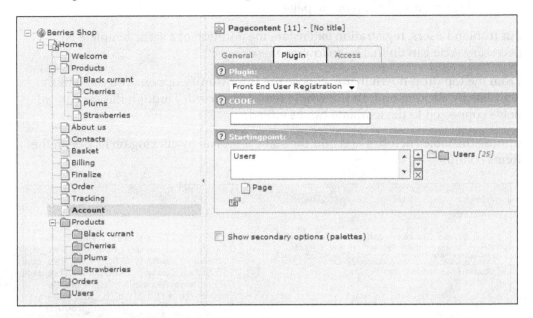

You should remember that for using **sr_feuser_register**, you also need extra extensions: **div2007** and **static_info_tables**. These extensions will be required in the sr_feuser_register installation process.

Also, you can use the extension tt_products for user registration. If you choose to use this extension for registering your online shop users, you need to configure TypoScript for this extension.

As in the previous example, create a SysFolder where the users' accounts data will be stored.

For the tt_products extension to be able to register new user accounts, you need to add the following code to the TypoScript configuration:

```
plugin.tt_products.createUsers = 1
```

Also, we set up some extra options in the setup field – setting up the group for a new user. Here we signed up these groups:

- Clients (with group ID 1)
- Trusted clients (with group ID 2)
- Administrator (with group ID 3)

For adding new users to clients, you need to add:

```
plugin.tt_products.memberOfGroup = 1
```

Also, specify the SysFolder ID where the new user accounts will be stored. New user accounts will be stored in this SysFolder:

```
plugin.tt_products.PIDuserFolder = 25
```

The new users will be sent e-mails with the username and password. The username will be the e-mail ID entered in the registration form, but the password will be generated automatically. At the same time, this data will be stored in your TYPO3 installation. The user can log into your web page with the received data. Also, you should remember that there aren't many avenues for adding user information using tt_products. If you want your users to be able to add detailed information about themselves, you should choose the sr_feuser_register extension. This extension provides the facility to add maximum information about the user. You can use this information in other parts of the web page - if you use an extension for a forum, for example.

For correct system operation, make sure that the accordant markers are in the created template file. For example, here is the code from `products_css_en.html.html` (the sample templates for tt_products are in `typo3conf/ext/tt_products/template`):

```
With your username and password it will be more convenient for you to
order at our shop!

Username: ###USERNAME###
Password: ###PASSWORD###

Please keep this e-mail in a secure place.
```

User identification and user accounts

The system extension **felogin** that provides user authentication is included in TYPO3. This extension provides registered users with authentication to your web page. For setting up this extension, you need to make a new content element and choose **Login** from the list, **Pagecontent**.

Add a title; and specify the page where the user will be redirected after authentication. If necessary, specify in the setup tab that the login form will be hidden after user identification.

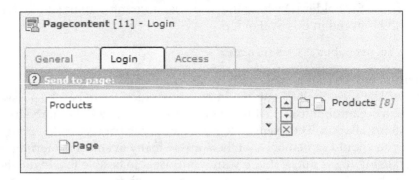

For editing users' data, you can use the sr_feuser_register extension, which provides user registration and data editing. For manually turning on the editing form, specify code **EDIT** in the configuration (you can find detailed information about the possible version of extension configuration in the official TYPO3 web page, and also read the sr_feuser_register manual—http://typo3.org/documentation/document-library/extension-manuals/sr_feuser_register/current/), as shown in the following screenshot:

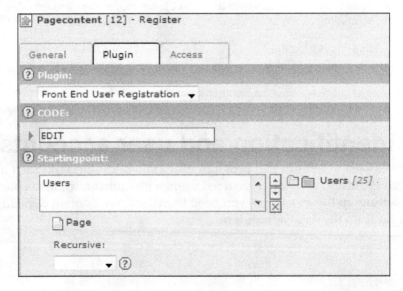

If you don't specify this, the code extension will automatically offer a registration form for users who aren't identified in the page (FE-User), or an editing form for those who are identified.

Dear, John Doe,
Edit the information of your membership **john.doe@webmail.com**

Please make sure that you fill in your details for the fields marked *

Click here to delete your membership.

Password:* ●●●●   Again: ●●●●

Name: **John**

Last name: **Doe**

Company:*   **Company Ltd.**

Address: **Imaginary Street 123**

City: **The City**

ZIP: **12345**

Telephone: **123456789123**

Fax: **123456789123**

E-mail:*   **john.doe@webmail.com**

WWW: **www.example.com**

Submit

Discounts for user groups

You can use the following methods to provide discounts for loyal clients:

- Using the discount field for each user. This option is available in the **Discount** field under the **Extended** table. You can set up discounts for each user individually.

- Using the field **price2**. You can see an example below of this field being used for discounts:

```
# ID of the FE user group
[usergroup = 1]
priceNoReseller = 2
[global]
```

- Using the calculation configured by TypoScript. You can see an example below of how to set up a discount for a product:

```
pricecalc {
    10.type = count
    10.field = price
    # Product with with ID 16 will be with 20% discount
    10.where = uid = 16
    # Full price is 1, so we set the 80% of full price
    10.prod.1 = 0.8
}
```

- Also, you can set up the discount depending on the number of product items in the basket (1 product costs 4.99, 2 products cost 8.99, and so on.):

```
pricecalc {
10.type = count
10.field = price
10.sql.where =
10.prod.1 = 4.99
10.prod.2 = 8.99
10.prod.5 = 19.99
}
```

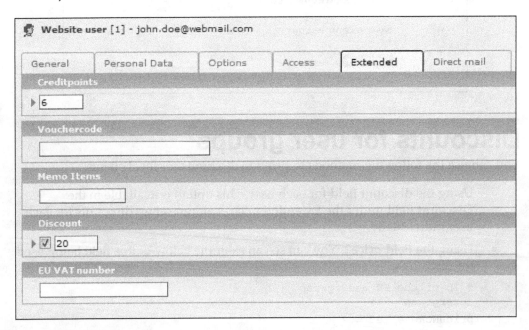

Using the discount field can take too much time because you have to enter these values individually. In this way, user discounts are difficult to overview. If a user amount grows, it then will be more difficult to administrate the discount values if you change it. You can use this method only for special VIP clients who need these values.

If you use field **price2**, you can specify a global value (user group) that will be used for clients' group discount calculation:

```
[usergroup = 1]
plugin.tt_products.priceNoReseller = 2
plugin.tt_products.getDiscountPrice = 1
[global]
plugin.tt_products.discountprice {
10.type = count
10.field = price2
10.additive = 0
10.sql.where =
10.prod.1 = 18.25
10.prod.10 = 17.04
}
```

Summary

In this chapter we explained that you might need the user register every day for growing your business, and also for promoting traffic and improving finances. Using a TYPO3-based online shop, you can offer discounts and campaign products that are just for registered users who are frequent customers. You can register users on your online shop in different ways that are more suitable for your web space.

In the next chapter we will describe navigation and searching possibilities inside shop content. The chapter describes how to organize common, supplementary, and linked content navigation.

6
Navigation Inside the Online Shop and Content Search

This chapter covers navigation and searching possibilities inside shop content. Navigation in your online shop is one of the most important aspects of creating an effective website. The web page design and content is also important but without navigation your website can't completely work. Navigation must be simple and logical; thereby, you can increase the number of visitors who will return to your online shop.

This chapter describes how to organize common, supplementary, and linked content navigation. The topics covered are:

- Navigation by products, producer, and other references
- Navigation types
- Additional extensions (indexed search)

By the end of this chapter, you should have navigation and searching integrated into the online shop catalogue and content.

Navigation inside page content and sitemap

Like most functions in your web page, navigation is also included in the TYPO3 Core. For example, navigation in TYPO3 offers different kinds of menus, searching fields, and also a searching system. All the menus that you need to create can be done using TypoScript configuration. The kind of menus might be:

- TMENU — text-based menus
- GMENU — graphical image menus for generating menus using font files (`*.otf`, `*.ttf`)
- HMENU — hierarchical menus
- IMGMENU — imagemap menus (using the tag `<area>`)

For a better understanding of how we can use these menus, we will survey the most frequently used examples separately — TMENU and GMENU. Note that HMENU is used for TMENU development. While developing HMENU, we didn't set up value `entryLevel = 1`; therefore, HMENU reads sitemap data from default — zero level.

TMENU

We can say that TMENU use is a matter of taste. The statement "graphical menu (GMENU) charge server" isn't true because every image for the graphical menu is created and cached on server. Therefore, images wouldn't be created anew with each page view.

For creating a simple TMENU menu, we can use code examples; this lets us create one of the simplest menus with one level without any separator and unlock the outdated `"onfocus="this.blur()"` parameter:

```
TOP-MENU = HMENU
  TOP-MENU {
  1 = TMENU
  1.wrap =
    1 {
    noBlur = 1
      NO{
      wrapItemAndSub = <span>|</span>
      allWrap = |*|  &#124; |*|
      }
```

The final result must be the text menu, as you can see in the following screenshot:

| 1st page | 2nd page | 3rd page | 4th page | 5th page |

GMENU

You can add visual elements or simple font files to graphical menus. The menu image will be generated from these elements. We can create a graphical menu like the one you can see in following screenshot:

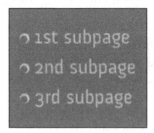

Code for this menu will look like this:

```
SIDEMENU = HMENU
SIDEMENU.entryLevel = 1
SIDEMENU.1 = GMENU
    SIDEMENU.1 {
    ### WRAP ALL MENU IN <ul> tag
    wrap = <ul>|</ul>
    noBlur = 1
        NO {
        wrap = <li class="menu">|</li> ### LIST (<li>) items class
        XY = [10.w]+23, 30
        format = gif
        backColor = #636363
        transparentColor = #636363
        1 = IMAGE
        ### SET THE DECORATIVE ELEMENT WITH IMAGE
        1.file = fileadmin/templates/img/leftgreen.png
        1.align = left
        1.offset = 5,8
        10 = TEXT
        10.text.field = title
```

```
     10.fontFile = fileadmin/fonts/anivers.ttf
     10.alttext.field = header // subheader
     10.fontSize = 20
     10.fontColor = #a2c83c
     10.offset = 20,18
     10.align = r
     }
  }
```

We created a menu that reads data from first level (not from base level); in this way, we created an unordered list menu with images that are decorated with an extra image. You can see in this example how a menu can be created with the default value "NO" but you can also supplement it using the value "ACT" for displaying individually active links.

Also, you can add some extra lines to GMENU using the field "subtitle". You can use this function if you need to add some information, for example, about "Products". Then, this subtitle could be "Our offer".

 Possible menu states are explained in more detail in the TypoScript reference documentation (tdoc_core_tsref), which you can find on the TYPO3 web page: http://typo3.org/ documentation/document-library/references/doc_ core_tsref/4.1.0/view/10/2/

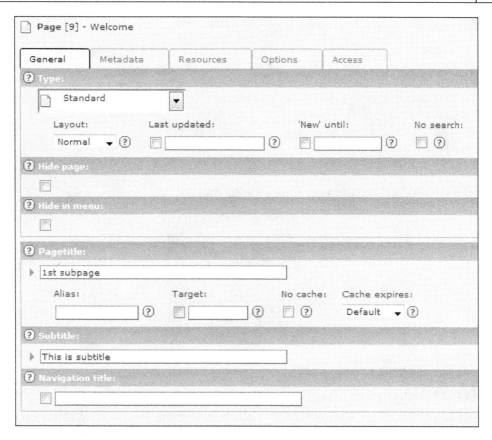

So, you can add an extra subtitle field for the menu name and provide more information for your online shop visitors. Also, your page visitors can find the necessary information faster:

```
10 = TEXT
10.text.field = title
10.fontFile = fileadmin/fonts/anivers.ttf
10.alttext.field = header // subheader
10.fontSize = 20
10.fontColor = #a2c83c
10.offset = 20,18
10.align = r
```

After typing these code lines, add some extra lines:

```
20 = TEXT
20.text.field = subtitle
20.fontFile = fileadmin/fonts/verdana.ttf
20.alttext.field = header // subheader
20.fontSize = 10
20.fontColor = #a2c83c
20.offset = 50,18
20.align = r
```

You can see the final result in the following screenshot:

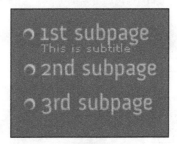

Sitemap

We can adjust the name **Sitemap** for two different but similar meaning elements of the web page. **Sitemap** is the site map of your website, with a chronological layout of the pages. This is a good way to help visitors understand the structure of your website. Also, **Sitemap** is in the XML format, where information about pages, page updates, and importance of pages is stored. The XML format site map is for search bots — for example Google or Yahoo! More detailed information about XML site map can be found in Chapter 9, where we describe SEO importance and requirements.

You can create a site map of your website and add this element to your online shop. Search bots will be able to find the sitemap and make a reference to your website.

Sitemap is available as a content element. You haven't set up any extra extensions for use as a site map element. For creating and adding **Sitemap** to your website, from the BE left menu, choose the **Page** module and also the page where the site map will be added. Press on **Create page content** and you can choose the new special element for your page content. In our example it is **Sitemap**, as you can see in the following image:

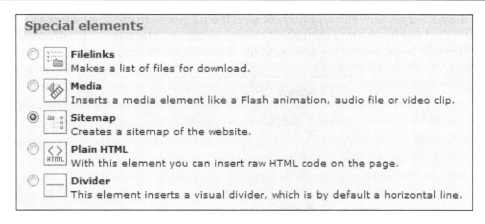

Add the necessary information in the offered form fields—for example, the title for this content element. Then, in the tab **Sitemap/Menu** choose:

- **Menu type—Sitemap**—as you see in the tab title, you can choose whether it will be an extra menu that is added like a content element.

- **Startingpoint**—point from where the page structure will be overseen.

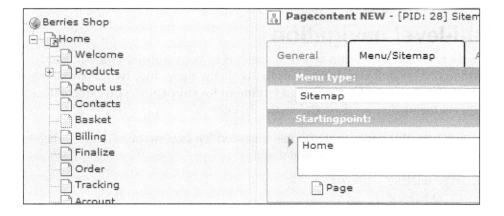

Save the added content element and click on the page where the site map was created. Call out the context menu and choose to oversee the page. The site map structure will be created using unsorted list tags (`<ul>`, `<li>` tags).

Multi-level navigation

Often, there can be a situation where for menus in your website you will need more than one level. If you don't want to divide the menu into two separate menus (for example, top menu for pages and left menu for subpages), you can create a multi-level menu.

For search bots, it is better that you use unsorted list tags (with `<ul>` `<li>` tags) because they are quiet similar to site map:

```
MULTILEVELMENU = HMENU
MULTILEVELMENU {
### FIRST LEVEL PAGES
    1 = TMENU
    1.wrap = <ul class="first-level">|</ul>
    1 {
        NO {
            wrapItemAndSub = <li>|</li>
        }
        ACT = 1
        ACT {
```

```
        wrapItemAndSub = <li class="first-level-sub active-link">|</
li>
        }
    }

    ### SECOND LEVEL PAGES (SUBPAGES)
    2 = TMENU
    2.wrap = <ul class="second-level">|</ul>
    2 {
        NO {
        wrapItemAndSub = <li>|</li>
        }
        ACT = 1
        ACT {
            wrapItemAndSub = <li class="second-level-sub active-link">|</
li>
        }
    }
}
```

In this example, we outputted the menu with two levels. If you need extra levels, you can add them using a part of the "SECOND LEVEL PAGES", as you can see in the code example below:

```
    ### SECOND LEVEL PAGES (SUBPAGES)
    3 = TMENU
    3.wrap = <ul class="third-level">|</ul>
    3 {
        NO {
        wrapItemAndSub = <li>|</li>
        }
        ACT = 1
        ACT {
            wrapItemAndSub = <li class="third-level-sub active-link">|</
li>
        }
    }
}
```

Usually, you can add submenus until the fourth level. But, you should remember that submenus are for page navigation improvement. You website menu levels should be friendly to online shop visitors.

Searching in TYPO3

You can use searching in TYPO3 without downloading any extra extensions. For this functionality in TYPO3, there is the system extension "indexed_search".

Search extension installation

You should switch to the Extension Manager for using this extension, as you can see in the following screenshot:

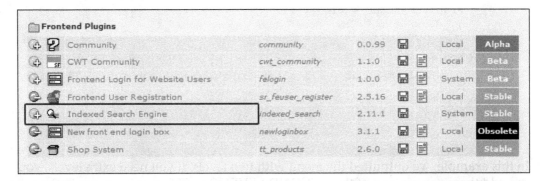

You need to install this extension by pressing the **+** icon next to the extension title **Indexed Search Engine**. Starting installation TYPO3 will inform you that the system couldn't find the **doc_indexed_search** extension. This extension includes documentation for searching extensions and you will be able to import it. You can import from the Extension Manager's side or by visiting the TYPO3 extension repository; from here it can be downloaded and installed without assistance.

You have two options at this stage: complete documentation installation or cancellation. Then, you can move on to the next step — importing the database's tables. This is required for searching the driver operation.

On the **Indexed Search Engine** extension installation, you will be able to manage the extension configuration, as you can see in the following screenshot:

```
CONFIGURATION:
(Notice: You may need to clear the cache after configuration of the extension. This is required if the extension adds T

  Path to PDF parsers [pdftools]
  The indexer uses the applications 'pdftotext' and 'pdfinfo' for extracting content from PDF files. These
  applications must be installed in this path. Otherwise leave the field empty.

  /usr/bin/

  PDF parsing mode [pdf_mode]
  Zero=whole file is indexed in one. Positive value: Indicates number of pages at a time, eg. "5" would
  mean 1-5,6-10,..... Negative integer would indicate (abs value) number of groups. Eg "3" groups of 10
  pages would be 1-4,5-8,9-10. Range is -100 to 100.

  20       (Integer)

  Path to unzip [unzip]
  The indexer uses "unzip" to extract the contents from OpenOffice.org/Oasis OpenDocument files. The
  application must be installed in this path. Otherwise leave the field empty.

  /usr/bin/

  Path to WORD parser [catdoc]
  The indexer uses the application 'catdoc' for extracting content from WORD files. The application must
  be installed in this path. Otherwise leave the field empty.

  /usr/bin/
```

Most of these options are for parse office documents using special software — for example catdoc, xlhtml, pdftotext, and pdfinfo (Xpdf).

If you specify this software location on your server, indexed searching can display the results as a plain text. Then, the changes are made and the chosen options are approved.

Adjusting the ABC template

Most people who use TYPO3 switch off comments using the TypoScript function. Therefore, we need to define for, which content will or will not be considered in our page.

If you don't specify it, the search results will display parts of menus, language menus, and unnecessary information.

To switch off comments that generate TYPO3 extensions, this TypoScript code can be used:

```
config.disablePrefixComment = 1
```

In this way, comments of element blocs and extensions will be taken from the page source.

```
<!-- CONTENT ELEMENT, uid:29/textpic [begin] -->
```

We use the HTML document. We add comments to the template showing where the block begins and where it ends; also, this comment specifies what the search needs to index:

```
<!--TYPO3SEARCH_begin-->
<!--TYPO3SEARCH_end-->
```

In our template it looks like this:

```
<!-- ###DOCUMENT_BODY### -->
<div class="container">
    <div class="header">
        <div class="logo">###LOGO###</div>
        <div class="topmenu">###TOP-MENU###</div>
        <div class="language">###LANGMENU###</div>
    </div>
    <div class="main">
        <div class="sidebar">###LEFT###</div>
        <!--TYPO3SEARCH_begin-->
        <div class="post">###CONTENT###</div>
        <!--TYPO3SEARCH_end-->
    </div>
    <div class="footer">###FOOTER###</div>
        </div>
</div>
<!-- ###DOCUMENT_BODY### -->
```

In our example, the ###DOCUMENT_BODY### marker marks the start and end of the template. This means that TYPO3 will ignore all the markers that are out of this marker field. All the necessary markers should be wrapped in this marker's borders.

You can choose another title for your website template's start and end markers; for example, ###BODY_CONTENT### and specify this title in the TypoScript configuration:

```
workOnSubpart = BODY_CONTENT
```

Accordingly, you need to add a line of TypoScript code in your page configuration. Then, you can use indexing in the page and the searching form will work:

```
page.config.index_enable = 1
```

Once the installation of the "indexed_search" extension is complete in the administrative section (Backend), you will see a new section called "Indexing" (under the base section "Admin tools").

The content gets indexed during the rendering of the pages, and content is not indexed if you are logged into the backend. To set up content indexing, you should visit your page from FE – this will trigger the indexing of page content.

If you do these steps correctly, your pages will be indexed.

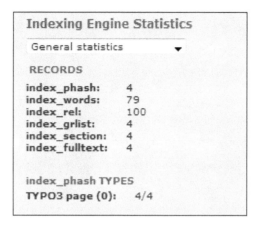

Adding search to the web page

Then, the extension is adjusted for our needs, which we can add in to the web page. You can add search functions like most of the extensions in TYPO3.

You need to create a new page or choose an existing page and add a **General Plugin**, as you can see in the following screenshot:

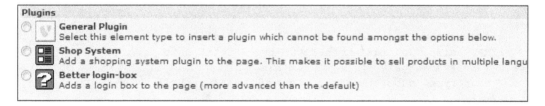

Choose "Indexed Search Engine" and save a new record. Visit your page from the FE side and test the new form in action.

Note that by default if you use the "indexed_search"extension indexing page, then you overlook these pages from the FE side. Therefore, the pages indexing takes place while you overlook, unless you are logged in to the back end. If you are logged in to the backend, your browsing of the frontend pages will not be indexed.

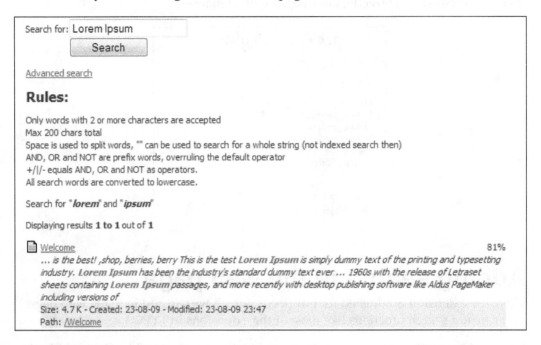

Using tt_products search, the extension template part ###ITEM_SEARCH### will be used:

```
<!-- ###ITEM_SEARCH### begin -
<form method="post" action="###FORM_URL###">
<INPUT size="30" maxlength="100" type="text" name="sword"
value="###SWORD###"/>
<input type="submit" name="order" value="Search"/>
</form>
<!-- ###ITEM_SEARCH### end -->
```

You should remember that this search field will not be used together or as a part of the indexed_search. Therefore, you can only use this field for a product item search.

If you need to use this searching form, add it into the page where the search is needed:

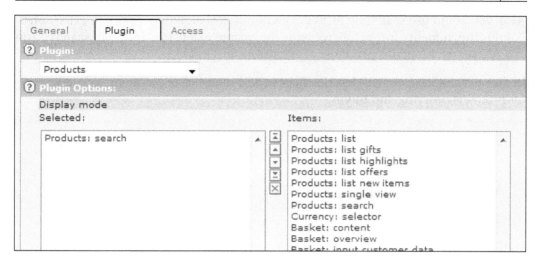

Specify the searching result page with TypoScript configuration; this will display the funded products and which fields will be used for the search.

```
plugin.tt_products.stdSearchFieldExt = title,subtitle,itemnumber
plugin.tt_products.PIDsearch = 8
```

Also, there is an alternative method; you can use the extension "indexed_search" together with the extension "crawler" on the understanding that you have SHELL/SSH command line access to your server. This way you could indicate forcibly a cHash value for table records, because tt_products does not offer this function at the moment.

Summary

Navigation is included in TYPO3 Core. The possible kinds of menus are TMENU, GMENU, HMENU, and IMGMENU. You can add an extra subtitle field for the menu name and provide more information for your online shop visitors.

If you need more than one level of menus, you can use the multi-level menu. It is tue that the multi-level menu is helpful for website visitors, but do not confuse them.

You can create a site map of your web page and use it to increase the functionality and efficiency of your website.

Also, you could use searching in TYPO3 without downloading any extra extensions. For this functionality in TYPO3, we have the system extension "indexed_search". You can add search functions like most of extensions in TYPO3.

In the next chapter, we will describe how to add modules of payment and delivery for products ordering and buying.

7
Ordering Organization—Modules of Payment and Delivery

This chapter describes how to add modules of payment and delivery for your products. Also, this chapter covers the safety aspects of ordering. For managing an online shop, you need a solution for processing these orders. Some extensions are necessary for managing orders from the backend side. But security certificates (SSL) become necessary when you are performing transactions using credit cards, which are very handy for your online shop visitors.

Topics covered in this chapter are:

- Modules of payment and delivery
- Use of SSL

By the end of this chapter, you will have configured add-ins for safe payment and products delivery.

Processing orders

If you are going to use your online shop not only as a web catalogue but also to allow customers to order products, then you need some solution to process these orders in your online shop.

The previously described extension "tt_products" already includes all the elements for your e-Commerce:

- Processing payments with PayPal, credit cards—additional extension modules are needed to accomplish this
- Processing orders FE (frontend)—change the order status, tracking

However, this solution is not enough and not handy for everyone. For example, products you should manage from the backend (administrative) side but orders you can manage from the frontend.

While we are writing this book, new and perspective extensions are available—for example "shop_manager" by Semyon Vyskubov. This extension is for tt_products, because it is necessary to manage orders from the backend side (like most of the options and resources) as you can see in the following screenshot:

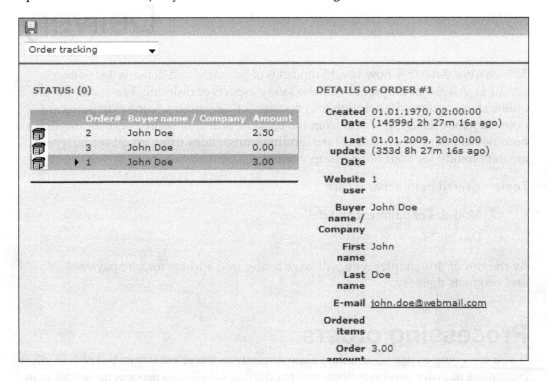

Using this extension, you can track the orders and also overlook "articles" and categories, in the same place.

For set up extension, download it from the TYPO3 TER (choose "shop_manager") — see Chapter 1 for an explanation of Extension Manager and the installation process for extensions. Also, you need to proceed with the standard set up procedure:

1. Go to Extension Manager.

2. Choose the saved extension copy from the web server HDD or import from the extension repository (TER).

3. Download it to your web space.

4. Configure the extension according to your site map (from the top drop-down menu, you should choose **Settings** and add the necessary information).

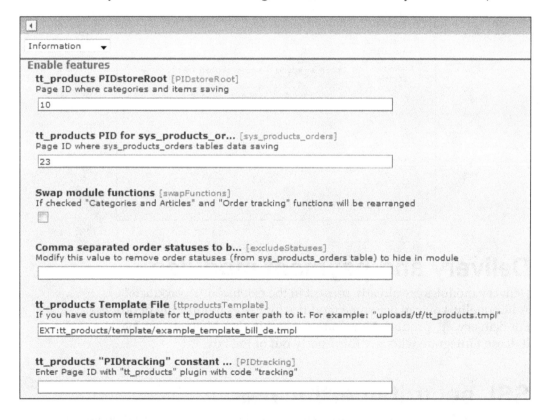

Operating with "shop_manager" is very easy. Using the available options you can change the status of the order. For example, if you have a new order and you wish to "receive" (change status), then the status of the order is changed to "receive" and the client is informed by e-mail that the products have been accepted.

You need to choose an order (orders are sorted by status—0 means that the order is received by the shop, but the administrator has not verified it yet) and make changes in the status option to "Accepted", as you can see in the following screenshot:

Delivery and payment modules

Delivery modules are already present in the extension "tt_products".
Additionally, you can use some modules for easier monitoring of orders.
For delivery, "tt_products" has some basic shipping/delivery settings, but
it doesn't integrate with any third-party out of the box.

SSL security certificates

SSL (Secure Sockets Layer) security certificates become necessary when you start
doing payments using credit cards. It is a common requirement of banks if you
cooperate with some of them, to provide payments with credit cards.

We can divide SSL certificates into two large categories according to the use of certificates:

- Identity certificates — the objective of these certificates is to inform whether the visitor whose address was typed into the input is on the web page.

- Encryption certificates — these protect the data between two computers (for example, between the online shop and visitor) so that all the data are confidential.

Also, TYPO3 users sometimes use SSL certificates for administrative side (backend) protection. This is possible using a web page provider's free SSL. Such certificates can be created using the open source solution OpenSSL.

But these certificates based on OpenSSL can be untrustworthy for web page visitors, because the certificate developer could be an unknown company. For web page users, it is necessary to identify the developer of the SSL certificate — this means that the certificate is really an SSL certificate and is secure. SSL should be installed on the server side for the following steps.

Remember that for your SSL certificate use, you have to install it. You should add certificates files (`*.crt` files) and private key files (`*.key`) to your web space. Also, you should configure the server, which for an Apache server will be like the example code below:

```
<VirtualHost 127.0.0.1:443>
    DocumentRoot C:/xampp/htdocs/berriesshop
    ServerName www.berriesshop.ltd
    SSLEngine on
    SSLCertificateFile /path/to/certificate.crt
    SSLCertificateKeyFile /path/to/key.key
    SSLCertificateChainFile /path/to/chain.crt
</VirtualHost>
```

For the correct SSL to work on your web space, carefully read the accordant server documentation:

- Apache SSL: http://www.apache-ssl.org/

- Windows IIS: http://support.microsoft.com/kb/299875

- Apache Mac OS X: http://developer.apple.com/internet/serverside/modssl.html

Configuring TYPO3 for SSL support

For SSL operating on a web server, accordant software is needed. For example, the Apache module is mod_ssl, which includes OpenSSL library or full OpenSSL software.

You can find detailed information on how to configure a server or virtual domain in the corresponding web server documentation.

For using TYPO3 with an SSL certificate for administrative side protection, go to the section "Install" or to your web page address:

```
http://www.example.com/typo3/install
```

From this address, you can move on to the "Install Tool" and activate some necessary options. The ENABLE_INSTALL_TOOL file in newer TYPO3 versions is available only for one hour (for security reasons). So, you should create this file manually — either through FTP client, or you can easily create the ENABLE_INSTALL_TOOL file from TYPO3 BE module **User Settings**. Use the **Create Install Tool Enable File** as shown in the following screenshot:

After the Install Tool access file is created, enter the Install Tool password — you can now access your TYPO3 options and configuration.

When the changes in the Install Tool are done, you can delete the ENABLE_INSTALL_TOOL file in this TYPO3 BE module.

For activating the SSL support from the TYPO3 side, you need to use a definite parameter, adding integral (int.) from 0 to 3 depending on the preferable impact:

```
[BE] [lockSSL] = 3
```

- 0 — function switched off
- 1 — https activated
- 2 — activated https scheme with visual http scheme
- 3 — forced https use

If the http protocol on the web server by default is not "443", you should change this parameter by adding the necessary port number at the end:

```
[BE][lockSSLPort] = 0
```

SSL extensions

We can assume that you will not need data encryption on every page. For example, you could use data encryption on the FE user's identification page for registry forms or to input sensitive bank/account information.

One solution is to use TypoScript and define the necessary pages with conditions. For easier management, you could use extra extensions from the TYPO3 repository, called "https_enforcer". With this extension, you can individually specify pages for which the https connection is necessary.

For pages requiring https, we can add such conditions in the constants:

```
[PIDinRootline = 12,19]
config.baseURL = https://www.berriesshop.ltd
[global]
```

This tells TYPO3 to set the html tag base URL for this page so that all the content on this page will be from the https' base URL.

Also, there are some extensions that can be useful.

There's a handy solution — the extra extension "https_enforcer" (Page HTTP/HTTPS Enforcer). This extension provides individual protocol management between http and https pages separately.

To use this extension:

1. Download it from the TYPO3 TER.
2. Install it through the Extension Manager.
3. Approve new tables for the database.
4. Perform extension configuration (it depends on the available options on your web page).

Detailed instructions on how to manage configurations are on the
TYPO3 web page: http://typo3.org/documentation/document-
library/extension-manuals/https_enforcer/current/

Using the extension "sm_httpscm" (Page HTTP/HTTPS Enforcer via Clickmenu),
you can add extra functions to the BE clickmenu (the menu that is shown when you
click the site tree) as you can see in the following screenshot:

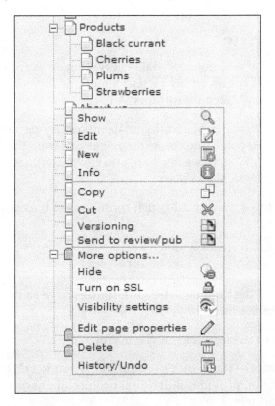

Payments

Chapter 3 explains how to add e-commerce plugins into an online shop that is based
on the TYPO3 CMS. Also, payments processing using the tt_products extension can
be realized with an extra extension called "paymentlib_paypal". This extension will
help to integrate the payment system for a PayPal account quickly and successfully.

The main PayPal service advantage is the possibility to accept and manage credit cards. If you are going to use bank systems with corresponding payment systems, you should remember that the integration can be complicated and takes time.

You could start using the extension "payment_paypal" by installing the following:

- The extra extension "static_info_tables" (for country codes, currency, and other information)

- A PayPal test account (recommended for testing gateway)

- A shop extention—in our in case, "tt_products"

If you use a PayPal account for processing payments, all the money will be stored in your PayPal account. Then, as and when required, you can transfer the money from the PayPal account to your bank account.

Also, PayPal is an extra safety guarantee for your transactions. Using PayPal reduces the risk of using useless credit cards in your online shop.

Summary

You need some solution for how to process orders in your online shop. New extensions are available—"shop_manager" by Semyon Vyskubov. This extension is for tt_products because it is necessary to manage orders from the backend side.

Delivery modules are already present in the extension "tt_products". SSL security certificates become necessary when you start to pay using credit cards.

Payments processing using the tt_products extension can be realized with the extra extension "paymentlib_paypal".

In the next chapter, we will describe the possibilities of administrating shop content using the administrative interface in TYPO3 BE.

8
Administrative Interface in TYPO3

This chapter covers the various options to administrate shop content using the administrative interface in TYPO3 BE (**backend**). In this chapter you will find will find a list of the available administrative functions, the different modules for content changes, and a description of the RTE extensions. The topics covered are:

- Adding, editing, and deleting records
- Different modules
- Recommendations for page functionality

By the end of this chapter, you should know the different options to administrate shop content, make changes, and get information from the administrative tools.

Available administrative functions

Sometimes a rash visual idea isn't realized using the system's additional functions. But nine times out of ten this visual idea can be realized using the extensions from the TYPO3 TER (TYPO3 extension repository). These can include many items, such as a teaser menu for content elements, galleries, and massive extensions like forums.

If you work with content changes on a day-to-day basis, you will use two kinds of modules: **Page** and **List**.

The **Page** module, as you can probably figure out from the name, is mostly used to oversee the page content and also layouts by columns and sequence.

The **List** module is handy in working with record lists, to oversee the records of new extensions for example. If you are using this module, supervising extension records becomes more effective.

Page module

The **Page** module is certainly convenient when you have to add new page content, make changes to existent content, or delete content. If you have a multilingual website, the **Page** module provides the content's records translation to different languages.

Using the drop-down menu, you can switch between modes:

- **Columns** (a view of page columns that you can see in the following image)
- **QuickEdit** (quick edit content by loading several positions together in one place: titles, texts, media)
- **Languages** (allows translations from the default website language to their previously configured language)
- **Page information** (shows information about page creation, last update data, and time)

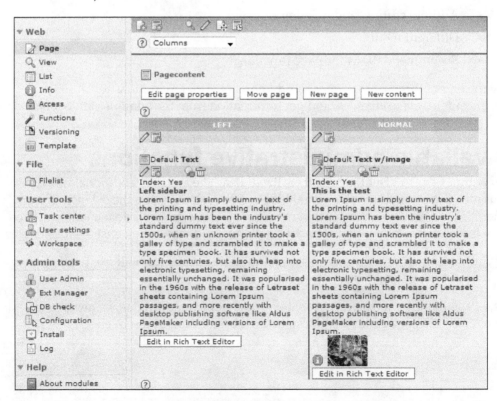

By the way, the tt_products extension isn't a standard event. The created records in the system folder can be viewed using the **List** module too. This is a facility provided by the author of the extension, which makes shop administrative functions easy. Not all extensions allow to monitor records with this module.

You can see the **Products** record view using the Page module, as seen in the following screenshot:

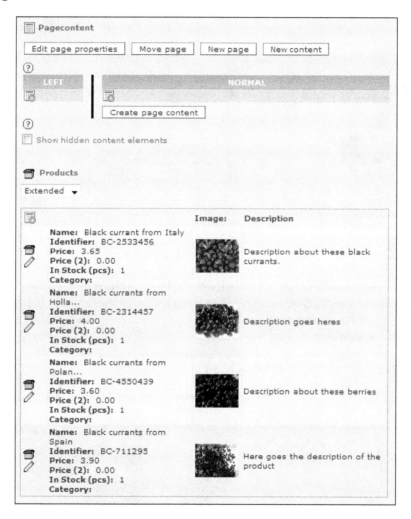

Using the tt_products extension through the List module, you can edit, add new products, or delete products.

List module

Using the List module, you can easily view records that are in the system folders. You can edit pages that contain content objects and extensions. Using the List module is tougher than using the Page module because you can't see the column's position before you open the record. You can see the Content elements in the List module, as shown in the following screenshot:

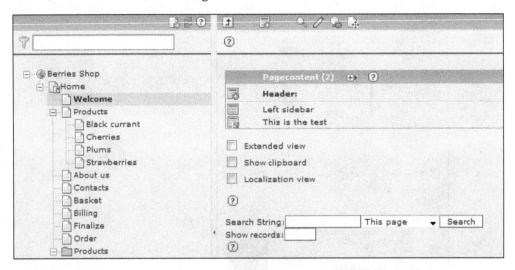

If you have to edit/add/delete records from the SysFolder, where you store product items and other records, choose **SysFolder** from the page menu and click on the icon with the **+** sign. Choose the necessary option from the drop-down menu, as shown in the following screenshot:

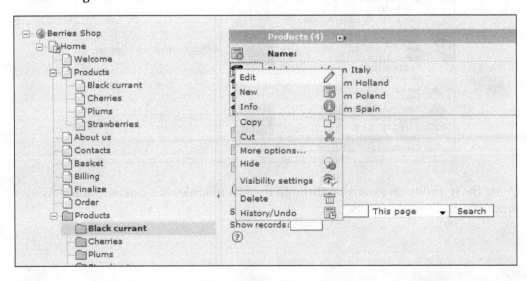

Info module

You can use this module to get information about page configuration, sitemap, and realized changes. If you switch the drop-down menu in the top-left corner, you can view the extra functions:

- **Page tree overview** — a page view where you can see the page base settings, page cache, and expiring. Also, in this overview, you can see if the page contains any extension's records — for example, in the product SysFolder, you can see the tt_products records.

- **Localization overview** — allows you to see pages with their translated versions if your web page is configured as multilingual (as you can see in the following screenshot):

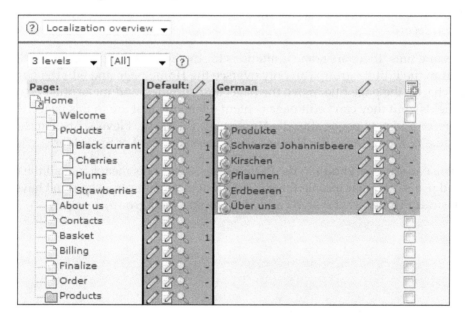

- **Log** — an overview of the realized changes in the definite page or in the whole sitemap if you are on the first level page.

- **Page TSconfig** — expands the page **TypoScript** configuration tree.

Extensions can extend the Info module. The Info module works as an extension base if a special backend module is developed. So this list can include other functions that the author of the extension will provide to output.

Access module

The Access module provides an overview of the user's accessibility to edit pages. Using TYPO3, you can limit page editing, deleting, or adding new pages. Accordingly, by adjusting the user's rights in TYPO3 backend, you can limit the user's ability to edit page records and content.

As you can see in the following screenshot, this is a **Permissions** view of the Access module. You can make changes here to limit or to allow access to pages for editing, deleting, and creating new ones, oversee existing pages, and also for editing page content.

You can see in the following image that the administrator (account: **edgars.karlsons**) created all the sitemap and is the owner of these pages. Administrative users, by default, can make all the changes in the page content or in the content items and extension records.

At the same time, there are some limitations for the **Editors** group. For example, users from the **Editors** group can only oversee the **Home** page and edit the page (this means change the page title, move the page, add subtitles, and make other changes in the fields), but they can't edit page content (elements that are in this page), delete the page, or add new pages after the **Home** page (in the next level). Also, these users can't add a new page after the **Home** page in the same level or SysFolder.

Also, you can see **Everybody** in the **Permissions** view. This means that all the other backend users can't manipulate the page content or page (users who don't have full administrator rights or who aren't added to the specified group).

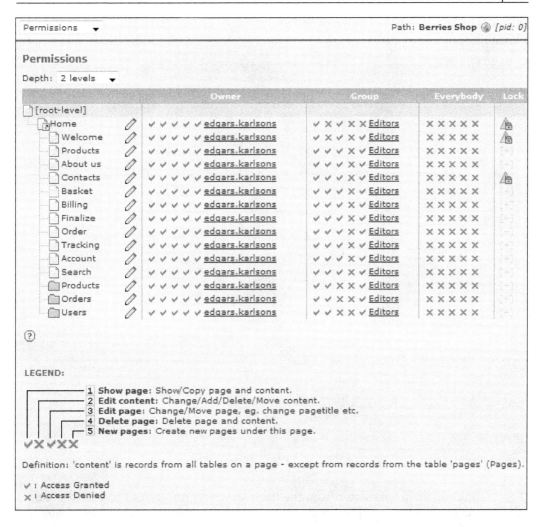

With **Lock**, you can limit all page manipulations for all those who don't have full administrator rights.

To make changes and to lock/unlock manipulation on a definite page, you should click on the red **X** symbol for connect access or on the green **V** symbol (tick) for disconnect access. Also, click on the + icon to lock the page.

If you want to see detailed information about page access rights, click on the pencil icon(s):

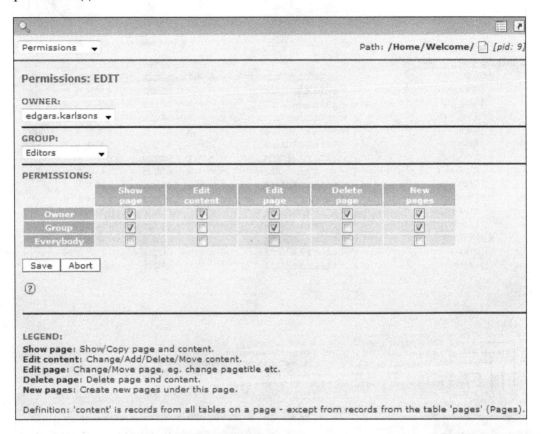

You can choose the page owner from the drop-down menu in this view. Also, you can choose the user groups if several are defined. After making the changes, save the page and pass onto the next page for editing page access rights if required.

Functions module

This module is scheduled for the creation of massive pages, for example, for the first pages in the sitemap. The Functions module can hold functions to provide more actions for a backend user. In the example for creating multiple pages, only one function is provided. If you enter page titles, up to nine new pages can be created, as you can see in the following screenshot.

Also, you can choose a **Wizard** that sorts pages in this module by the following:

- Page title
- Subtitle
- Change time
- Create time

Versioning module

In the Versioning module, you can manage created records in the Draft and Live environment, verifying or refusing records accordingly. You can use this module if you don't want to allow any of the users to edit the website's Live (online) version. You can use the Versioning module if the users prepare records. Then you can verify these records and publish in the page's Live version or refuse these records and leave them for editing and changing.

Template module

We already worked in this module and added a template for the online shop and web page. If you are using an extension that is written through the **Constants** file, you can reach it by using the **Constants Editor** submodule. The file that provides easy extension configuration and contains the main values for extension configuration is Constants.txt.

Filelist module

Using the Filelist module, you can access and change files that are in the `fileadmin` folder, as you can see in the following screenshot. There is data in the `fileadmin` folder for:

- Templates: HTML, CSS, and graphical images

- Font files: GFX headers or GMENU (graphical menu)

- Images for web pages: if you don't add images through the Page module upload (storing images in the folder `/uploads` or if you are using upload through extension—storing images in the folder `/uploads/ tx_extensionname/`).

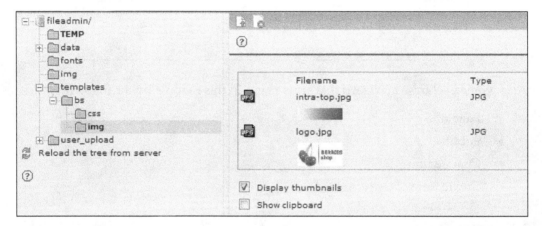

User settings

You can make changes in this module for your backend user account—change the username, password, name and surname, e-mail, language (if you have an added translation, for example, in German) as you can see in the following screenshot:

(?)

User Settings - Edgars Karlsons [edgars.karlsons]

| Language & Personal data | Startup | Edit & Advanced functions | Admin functions |

Your name: Edgars Karlsons

Your email address: edgars.karlsons@netberries.lv

Notify me by email, when somebody logs in
from my account: (edgars.karlsons@netberries.lv)

New password:

New password, again:

Language: English ▾

| Save Configuration | Reset all Values to default | (?)

ADMIN CONTROL FOR RE-ENABLING INSTALL TOOL ACCESS
By clicking this button, a file typo3conf/ENABLE_INSTALL_TOOL is created (or removed if it already exists).
It unlocks the access to the Install Tool (password is still needed!) and will be removed automatically after 1 hou

| Create Install Tool Enable File |

Notice! In order to activate most of these changes, please reload the backend (eg. logout and login again).

If you have administrator rights, you can create or delete the **ENABLE_INSTALL_ TOOL** file in this module. The **ENABLE_INSTALL_TOOL** file provides you access to the **Install Tool**. If this file has been deleted or created 60 (or more) minutes ago, you can't access the Install Tool.

User Admin module

Users who have administrative rights could make changes in their own and in other backend users' accounts in this module.

You can add a new user, delete unwanted users, add priority to users, or limit the rights—for example, you can limit access to some backend modules, languages, and domains (you can also administrate several domains and sub-domains with one TYPO3 installation).

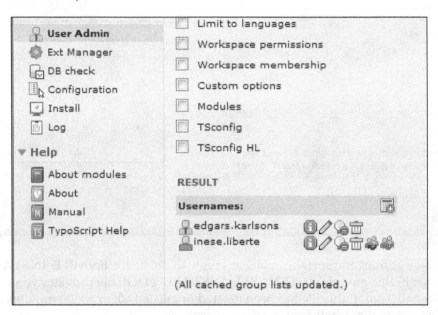

If backend users are large in number, it is more effective to create a **Backend usergroup** where you can add users with the same access rights. By using **Backend usergroup**, you will save lots of time not having to edit access rights to each user individually. You can add users with the same access rights to the **Backend usergroup** and, if necessary, configure the rights to a group that will refer to all the users in this group.

To create a new user group, choose the **List** module and site root page. Click on the **+** icon for a new record, as you can see in the following screenshot:

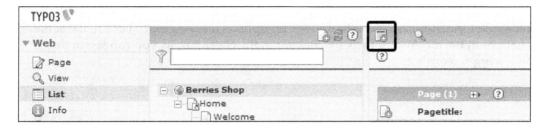

Choose **Backend usergroup** to create a new group:

To create a new group, it is enough to just set up a group name. But you should remember that it is also important to set up options for the group. Let's make some changes in the tab **Access Lists** by clicking in the checkbox, as you can see in the following screenshot:

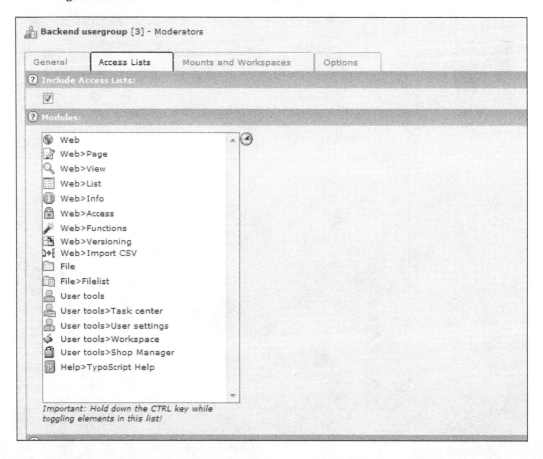

You can use the following sections for the actions given:

- Modules—by checking specific modules (hold down the *Ctrl* key to check multiple items), you will choose which modules will be seen by users who are in the defined group.

- Tables (listing)—by checking specific tables (content tables and extension tables), you will choose which tables will be accessible for the group's users for checking.

- Tables (modify)—by checking specific tables (content tables and extension tables), you will choose which tables will be accessible for the group's users for editing or adding items.

- Page types—will provide that user group with access to specified types of pages. For example, in a bad situation, a user who does not have a limit over choosing types of pages can change the page type to "sysfolder". TYPO3 doesn't display SysFolder like a page but uses it for data storage, so this modified page will not be seen. You can prevent that kind of incident using the Access module where you can limit the page edit.

- Allowed excludefields—connect fields that are not for standard users without full administrator access. If some extensions have a field in the form that is accessible only for administrator editing, choosing this field editing rights will also get group members.

- Explicitly allow/deny field values—this list includes different kinds of content elements (image, text with image, frontend user registration, among others). You can limit access to these elements, namely banning creation of specified content elements in the page. This list can be modified, depending on the extensions that are installed on your TYPO3-based web page.

You can choose a page (or several pages) in the next tab **Mounts and Workspaces** from where the site tree will be overseen (adding site root starting point). If you didn't set this page, users without administrator rights will not be able to see the site tree at all.

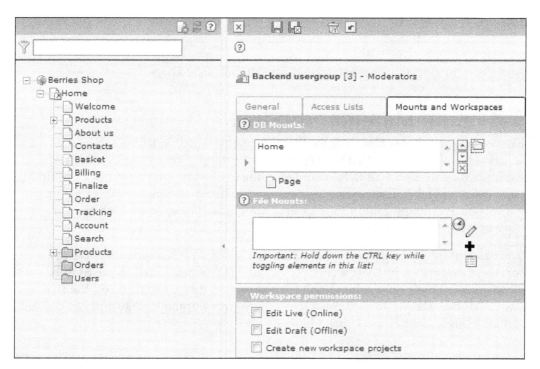

If you add the first-level page, all subpages will be seen. But if you want to limit the group's members, you can choose some separate pages.

After making all the changes, save the group. You can move on to editing user data or creating a new user. Also, you can add users to the created group.

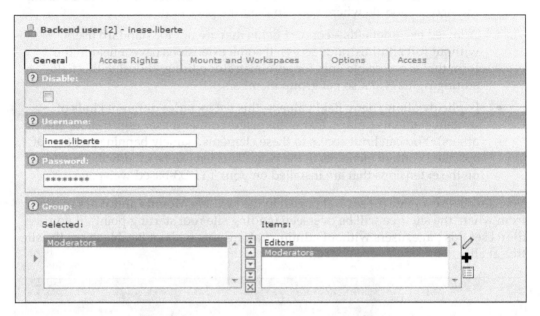

Add the created user group to backend users and save changes.

Extention Manager module

Extensions provide expansion of the TYPO3 functionality. So if you need a new function for your website that is not provided by the TYPO3 sysext (System Extensions—extensions already included in the CMS system), you should use an extra extension for it. Each extension can provide different functionalities—from a guest book and image gallery to large and complicated extensions such as online shop extensions or forums.

You can find more than a thousand extensions in the TYPO3 repository. We can sort these extensions by their security level, so it is recommended to use **Stable** extensions as much as possible. Don't use extensions that are marked **on the live site** or **Alpha** because these extensions are in the development stage and can contain errors or bugs.

You can use several functions in the Extension Manager module:

- Loaded extensions — a list with loaded extensions. You can add these extensions to pages if necessary. If you added an extension and don't see it in this list, check if you installed this extension — switching to the **Install extensions** mode.

- Install extensions — a list with extensions that are uploaded to the /typo3conf/ folder (where local extensions are stored — manually added) or to the /typo3/ext/ folder (system extensions that are present along with TYPO3 but may not be installed). For extension installation, you should click on the **+** icon near the extension title.

- Import extensions — this function provides the ability to download new extensions to your TYPO3 installation from the TYPO3 extension repository. If you don't change the **Settings** function, by default only reviewed extensions will be available.

- Translation handling — in our example, we have two languages: English (default) and German. Choose the required language and check if the translation is available on the TYPO3 translation server (http://translation.typo3.org/) for using multilingual page content (translations of extensions and backend interface translations). If the existing translation is incomplete for the language you require, or there isn't a translation for the required extension, you have two choices:
    - Volunteer as a TYPO3 core/extension translator and make the translations on the translation server.
    - Download the extra extension for translations — **llxmltranslate** — so that you can make a label localization.

- Settings (TYPO3 extension repository) — if you are developing your own extensions, you can specify access to your account in the TYPO3 page for adding extensions to the common TYPO3 TER.

- Check for extension updates — provides a function to check if there are any updates for the extensions in use on your page. As an alternative, we recommend using the extension **ter_update_check** or **ch_lightem**, which makes it easier to find and replace outdated extensions.

DB check module

The DB check module is for statistical and database checkups. Often this module is used for checking and updating the global reference index. This module's available functions are:

- Records Statistics—displays different statistics for a database (for example, you can see the created product items).

- The Page Tree—displays all the created pages in the tree. You should remember that without additional actions, TYPO3 doesn't delete database records—the system only marks records as deleted.

- Relations (checks table content for databases, empty tables, and so on)—this function can be used in a situation where you need to check the linked files to records (for example, an unnecessary record can be deleted but an image might refer to that deleted record):

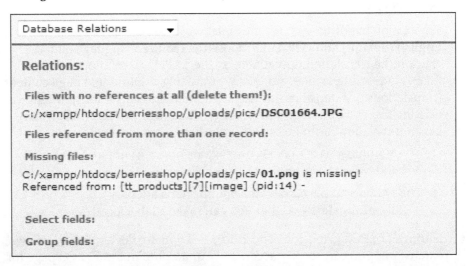

- Search Whole Database (searching for a specific record and table in the database)—this function is useful when you are looking for some specific records, but can only remember some details from those records—a specific word, file name, or other details.

- Search all filenames for a pattern—following the default example (\.php[3-6]?(\..*)?$|^\.htaccess$) find all the *.php and .htaccess files that are in subdirectories related to the page root folder. You can find detailed information about regex (or regexp) at: http://www.php.net/manual/en/ref.regex.php

- Check and update the global reference index—allows to check reference in the database and restore index for used functions.

Configuration module

Using this module, you can access the TYPO3 CMS configuration in the reading mode. For example, if you have to make changes in the `localconf.php` file, you can create the accordant configuration in this module and copy this configuration to the file manually.

Install module

This module allows access to the Install module. It is like using the URL: `http://www.example.com/typo3/install/`.

If you are working on TYPO3 that is already installed and the installation is complete, you can access the TYPO3 Install Tool through this module with some necessary manipulations. For using this function, you should have access to the **ENABLE_INSTALL_TOOL** file in the `/typo3config/` folder.

Log module

You can see the log access information, changes, error notifications, and successful/unsuccessful authorization attempts in this module. With this module, you can follow all the actions that are made in TYPO3. Also, this module tracks unauthorized access to the TYPO3 backend with username and password guessing. Log module tracks added, deleted, or edited records in the database. This is a handy way to follow your web page to see all the actions that are going on. The Log module is an alternative to the admin dashboard `*.log` file—if these are available on your web server.

Administration log

Users: All users ▾   Max: 20 ▾
Time: No limit ▾   Action: All ▾

30-01-10

Time	User	Type	Error	Action	Details
23:51	edgars.karlsons@LIVE	SETTING		Change	Personal settings changed (msg#254.1.1)
23:50	edgars.karlsons@-99	LOGIN		LOGIN	User edgars.karlsons logged in from 127.0.0.1 () (msg#255.1.1)

21-12-09

Time	User	Type	Error	Action	Details
04:08	edgars.karlsons@-99	LOGIN		LOGIN	User edgars.karlsons logged in from 127.0.0.1 () (msg#255.1.1)

Help module

The Help module includes information about all the submodules that are provided for information output on your TYPO3 installation. Here you can find information about TYPO3: from who the system creators are (Kasper Skårhøj is the project founder) to the inline manual. This manual describes, step-by-step, the accessible functions from a beginner's user level to a professional's user level of TYPO3 (use of specific functions).

The Help module contains submodules such as the following:

- About modules (short descriptions of modules)
- About (information about TYPO3 CMS and installed extensions)
- Manual (contains an Inline User Manual about TYPO3 functions and how to use these functions)
- TypoSript Help (TSREF—TypoScript reference, USER TSCONFIG—User TypoScript configuration, and PAGE TSCONFIG—Page TypoScript configuration).

RTE (Rich Text Editor) extension

RTE is an extension of the TYPO3 system that is added to the TYPO3 package. RTE is a kind of **WYSIWYG** ("What You See Is What You Get") text editor. RTE provides similar functionality to rich text editors like OpenOffice Writer or Microsoft Office Word.

We can call extension **rtehtmlarea** as one of the important extensions in TYPO3. But this extension has some replacements, such as the following:

- tinyRTE (tinyrte)—Rich Text Editor based on TinyMCE
- tinymce_rte (tinymce_rte)—Rich Text Editor again based on TinyMCE, but this extension is more advanced and has a newer version. We can say that the general advantage of this text editor is there are more possibilities to manipulate tables that are created using this extension. You can include class, colors, borders, custom column widths, and do other manipulations with tables.

TYPO3 RTE provides functions such as formatting with bold, italic, underline, adding headers, paragraphs, line breaks, or adding images and tables to the text. You can choose different RTE configurations—Basic, Advanced, or Custom, which you can manage in the Ext Manager extension settings.

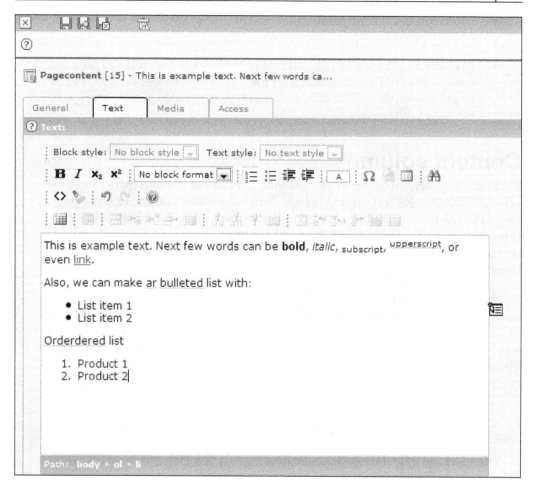

Backend interface and configuration

As we mentioned before, using TypoScript, you can manage not only template configuration but also adjust the backend layout and view. We should note some common examples that can facilitate and improve work with TYPO3. These examples are:

- Content column options—amount and arrangement. For example, if you use a template that contains one or two columns, you also see one or two columns in the backend, but not four.

- Content element input fields' configuration—for example, if you want to remove an input field because you don't need this field and always leave it empty.

- Extension fields configuration
- RTE (WYSIWYG text editor) configuration, stylesheets, advanced options
- And other options that you can find in the TYPO3 TSconfig (TypoScript configuration) documentations on the TYPO3 web page: `http://typo3.org/documentation/document-library/references/doc_core_tsconfig/current`

Content columns

There are four default content columns that you can see without extra options— LEFT, NORMAL, RIGHT, and BORDER. This means that you can create a page template down to four columns. Also, you can use extensions that provide the possibility to add extra columns. Prevalent in these are nested columns where one column is split into several subcolumns. Also, if you use the TemplaVoila! template system, you can create as many columns as you need.

All the options that are seen below should be entered by you in the root page configuration (so that they will be visible in the backend), but not in the Template module (where the TypoScript configuration is added—information from TypoScript will be visible in your web page frontend. This means that the information will be visible to online shop visitors).

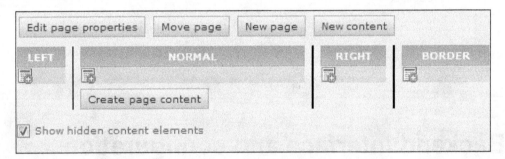

So, originally, you have four columns and each column has its own ID. You can use this ID for configuring the amount and arrangement of columns:

- **NORMAL** column: 0
- **LEFT** column: 1
- **RIGHT** column: 2
- **BORDER** column: 3

If you need the end result to show two columns — **LEFT** and **NORMAL** — you should use the code like this:

```
mod.SHARED.colPos_list= 1,0
```

And you'll see the output in the backend, as shown in the following screenshot:

You can add the columns IDs as you need, according to the arrangement and amount. For example, arrangement can be similar to the code below (NORMAL-LEFT-RIGHT):

```
mod.SHARED.colPos_list= 0,1,2
```

Headings and content elements

It is possible that one of the necessary functions is the option to choose heading tag style for content elements like h1, h2, h3, and others. TYPO3 provides this option. If you use these tags, the result for your web page search will be better in search engines like Yahoo! and Google. If you use the heading tags, you specify page content importance in a hierarchy.

A good example is that you can use the h1 tag together with logotype or slogan line and hide it using CSS:

```
h1 {
    text-indent: -9999px;
}
```

If you create a new content element by default, TYPO3 will offer prepared heading examples, as you can see in the following screenshot:

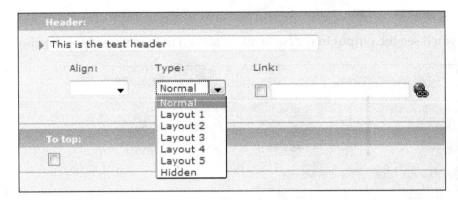

You can see that the attributes **Layout 1**, **Layout 2**, and so on are not self-explanatory. So, you can specify what they mean with the following configuration:

```
TCEFORM.tt_content.header_layout {
    altLabels {
            # Let's rename the headings with h1, h2 and h3 tags
        0 = Page main heading (H1)
        1 =
        2 = Page subheading (H2)
        3 = Page subheading (H3)
        4 =
        5 =
        }
    # Remove the unneeded Layout types
    removeItems = 1,4,5
}
```

Save the configuration and see the results of adding a new record or editing the existing ones, as you can see in the following screenshot:

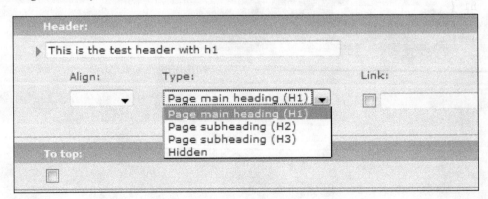

Titles that are outputted in the frontend will be corresponding and friendly to search engines. Titles will be marked following these hierarchies. In the following screenshot, you can see the result of the output in frontend, which depending on your CSS configuration (font size, color, and so on) looks like this:

This is the test header (h1 tag)

Lorem Ipsum is simply dummy text of the printing and typesetting industry. Lorem Ipsum has been the industry's standard dummy text ever since the 1500s, when an unknown printer took a galley of type and scrambled it to make a type specimen book.

And now for something completely different (h2 tag)

A few words about tests goes here...

The last one (h3 tag)

It has survived not only five centuries, but also the leap into electronic typesetting, remaining essentially unchanged. It was popularised in the 1960s with the release of Letraset sheets containing Lorem Ipsum passages, and more recently with desktop publishing software like Aldus PageMaker including versions of Lorem Ipsum.

You can see one more field in the content element window where you add a new record. This field is named **Frame**. You can easily use this field if you need to wrap the record into a defined element or element class. For this you can also use special formatted elements, such as another background color, text size, record width, and so on. So, you can use these options when you need to format special elements in your online shop.

To make changes in this field, in the root page **Options**, add the following TypoScript configuration (we will specify two values: for a record that is 50% wide and for a wrapper record for special notes):

```
TCEFORM.tt_content.section_frame {
    # Remove default items
    removeItems = 1,5,6,10,11,12,20,21
    # Add new items
    addItems.40 = 50% wide entry
    addItems.41 = Important (With red text)
}
```

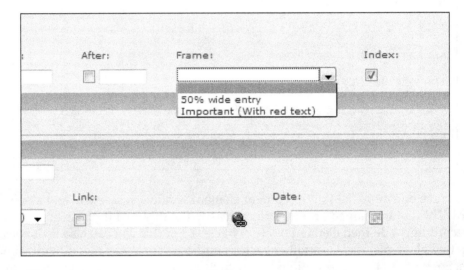

Also, in the template section, you need to add configuration that contains code with values, which should be the output for page visitors in one or another case:

```
### SECTION FRAME WRAPPER
tt_content.stdWrap.innerWrap.cObject = CASE
tt_content.stdWrap.innerWrap.cObject {
  key.field = section_frame
  40 = TEXT
  40.value = <div class="50percent-wide">|</div>
  41 = TEXT
  41.value = <div class="important-wrap">|</div>
}
```

In this way, a record with value "Frame" - "50% wide entry" will be wrapped with the class 50percent-wide. Also, it is important to specify class 50percent-wide view in the CSS file.

TCEFORM

Here are some of the options you can use in TCEFORM.

Fields switch off

This is when you don't use or need a field—frequently, you leave it empty. Also, there could be a situation when you need to limit the access to some fields in your online shop backend. It is possible to manage these options with TypoScript. Using TCEFORM, you can switch off fields for:

- Pages
- Extension's records
- Default content elements

In the following example we can see which fields are specified:

```
TCEFORM.pages{
  header_position.disabled = 1
  spaceBefore.disabled = 1
  spaceAfter.disabled = 1
  selectionIndex.disabled = 1
  layout.disabled = 1
  cache_timeout.disabled = 1
  no_cache.disabled = 1
  no_search.disabled = 1
}
TCEFORM.tt_products {
    subtitle.disabled = 1 # Disable subtitle field
    www.disabled = 1 # Disable WWW field
    price2.disabled = 1 # Disable Price2 field
    tax.disabled = 1 # Disable Tax
    weight.disabled = 1 # Disable Weight
    note2.disabled = 1 # Disable Note field
    datasheet.disabled = 1 # Disable Datasheet field
}
```

So, these fields will be switched off in the **Page** options. Also, some fields will be switched off in the extension tt_products. You can see the result in the following screenshot.:

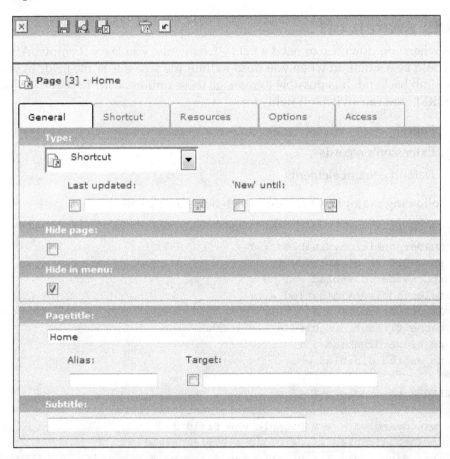

You can find more examples about TCEFORM (and page TSconfig) configuration in the TYPO3 TSref documentation: `http://typo3.org/documentation/document-library/references/doc_core_tsconfig/current`.

Summary

TYPO3 provides flexibility of information flow and replacement. TYPO3 has a lot of modules that can be used for different requirements.

RTE is an extension of the TYPO3 system that is added to the TYPO3 package. RTE provides functionalities that are similar to those of most rich text editors like OpenOffice Writer or Microsoft Office Word.

It is very useful that with TYPO3 you can manage template configuration and also adjust backend layout and view. Another powerful function is TCEFORM, with which you can switch off unnecessary fields such as pages, extension's records, and default content elements.

In the next chapter, we will describe online shop web page optimization corresponding to SEO requirements, and explain how to get popular on search engines.

9
Online Shop SEO Development

This chapter covers online shop web page optimization corresponding to SEO (Search engine optimization) requirements and how to increase prominence within search results. Several things determine the effectiveness of SEO (that is, how to ensure that your web page would be easy to find on the Internet); nevertheless there are not many basic principles of SEO. It is possible to achieve good results by using just a few simple techniques.

The topics covered in this chapter are:

- Title tags
- Keyword selection
- Page content and description
- Anchor text
- Some extensions for SEO

By the end of this chapter, you should know how to structure content and modify web page source for powerful SEO results.

The importance of SEO

As important as it is to create a visually attractive web page with all the necessary functions that allow finding information about the company — in our case, where to buy berries — it is important to take some steps so that the online shop can be found on the Internet.

SEO (Search Engine Optimization) is an important activity to make a web page effective and profitable (to be indexed in search engines like Google, Bing, and Yahoo!, among others). Sometimes SEO is called searching optimization, but this is still just a series of steps that result in an optimized web page being shown higher on the search result list when searching for specific **keywords**, such as "berries sale", "buy currants", or "berries wholesale".

The fundamental principle of optimizing a web page is smartly choosing the web page structure (menus, and sub-links, as well as the general structure of the page) in the early stages of development. It is important to note that the successful technical development of the page alone does not ensure a high number of visits for your online shop. The following aspects are essential for the successful indexing of a web page—these will affect the presence of your web page on the Internet:

- The incoming links from other websites—it is recommended that the linked web pages are from a similar industry

- Categorizing—this is the optimal solution for building the basic navigation of a web page

- The context of the content (the density and the consistency of topics)—that is, a page containing one topic rather than, say, four topics will be indexed more successfully

Google is currently the most popular search engine. This is also one of the most visited web pages in the world. The address for the international page of Google is www.google.com.

Most likely, the potential visitors of an online shop will use Google to search for information about goods available in your shop. It is necessary to know the basic principles of SEO and the use of those principles so that your online shop can easily be found according to its characteristic keywords.

Professionally implemented SEO requires relatively large amounts of financial resources and time. Sometimes the cost of such optimization exceeds the cost of traditional advertising. Nevertheless, SEO is a long term investment; it can effectively ensure that a web page is among the top 10-50 Google search results for several years.

Moreover, if your web page has a successfully planned structure, the site links will be shown under the title of your web page in the results of the search engine. This will allow the visitor of your page to access directly the information he/she is searching for (for example, books, music, and so on). This can be seen in the following image:

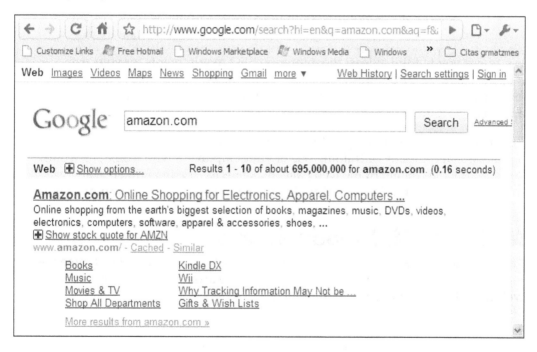

By default, Google displays ten search results per page. Research shows that people browse the first 3-5 Google pages, provided that the information searched is important. But if the information is less important or there are some time constraints, only the first 10-15 search results are viewed.

Depending on the specific country, the potential visitors of a web page have an option to do the Google search within national boundaries, taking the language (for example, French, German, among others) of a web page into consideration. Your SEO can be more effective if your target audience is the population of a certain country. There are fewer hits per keyword within one country than there is on the whole world wide web.

Implementing SEO solutions

The implemented SEO principles can be divided into three groups:

- Minimum (technical) SEO requirements—the implementation of which does not require much time or specific knowledge

- Optimal SEO requirements (categorization, successful page structure)—requires more time and a certain amount of knowledge

- Long-term SEO—requires continuous work with the website content in order to achieve good Google search results and to maintain them

We advise you to fulfil at least the minimum SEO requirements for your web page. The optimal SEO requirements can be fulfilled in the course of time along with developing the popularity of your online shop and with traditional advertising activities.

But in order to fulfil long-term SEO requirements, we advise using the services of a professional company or training one of your employees who would, on a daily basis, follow the content of the web page, make necessary amendments, analyze the effectiveness of the SEO principles' implementation, and make improvements.

Minimum SEO requirements

The minimal SEO requirements are the technical side of web page development—the menus that are formed as lists, footer links, and the arrangement of the content of the web page. The minimum SEO requirements include:

- Technical requirements
- The minimal requirements for website content

Technical requirements

To improve the results of SEO, we advise the following technical solutions:

- Use tables only for data that requires the use of tables. You should note that tables are for table data and not for content elements with information.

- Make sure that your website works correctly on different browsers.

- Enable an option that allows the search system robots to scan the links of your website without session identification and arguments that allow tracing the route within the limits of the website.

- Make sure that your website maintenance server supports the HTTP header "If-Modified-Since". This gives Google the information on whether any modifications have been made since the last scanning of the website by Google system.

- With respect to TYPO3, the search engines can correctly read the websites created on this CMS—both the parts of the website and the internal links.

For the best SEO result, it is necessary to include several aspects: first, creating the content of the website that corresponds to the goals of the website and the availability of products; and second, observing the technical requirements with respect to the clarity of programming code and those attributes that influence the overall rating of a website for the search engines.

But just as important are the ratings of the websites that link to your website. These can improve the rating or your website (and thus place it higher in the search results), but it can also spoil it.

The minimal requirements for website content

The simplest way to ensure that more potential customers visit your website is to inform them about this website on the Internet. It is also possible to create a link to your online shop in any other web page. This in general will improve the rating of your website.

We advise you to create links to your online shop only in web pages of relevant businesses. Ensure the following about your web page:

- We suggest creating references (links) to your online shop only in web pages from the same industry as your web page. The information that your web page contains has to fit the general concept of your web page.

- The information has to be easy to understand (preferably laconic, lacking any irrelevant information. If there is a lot of information, it has to be placed in the web page while keeping in mind how the visitors of the web page will find and perceive it).
- The information also has to be useful for the visitor.

Your website is primarily meant for its visitors. By creating useful and clear content and observing also the optimal SEO requirements, the website can be adjusted to fit the needs of search engines.

Optimal SEO requirements

Along with the minimal SEO requirements, it is advisable to observe the requirements described in this section. The optimal SEO requirements for ensuring effective SEO can be divided as follows:

- Requirements for content of the website
- The solutions provided by Google

Requirements for content of the website

To improve the possibility of finding your website according to specific keywords, we advise you to observe the principles that relate to the requirements about the content of the website as well as the technical requirements. The main requirements for the content are as follows:

- The text in your website should be created so that it includes most of keywords which the customer will be able to find your online shop through.
- The most important titles and words should be created as text (not as images or graphical elements). Google does not recognize an image as such. Therefore, use the attribute <Alt> to describe images.
- The information of tag <title> and attribute <Alt> should precisely describe the content and meaning of the web page or image.
- Do not include too many keywords and words describing your website in the tag <keywords>. It is recommended to have not more than twenty keywords on one page.
- Create a map of your website for the convenience of the visitors.
- Within the limits of the website, create internal textual links. The number of such links should not be too high, but there should be at least one link to each part of the website. Make sure that all the links are working.

When adding content to your existing page or when creating a new page, you can ensure the fulfilment of basic SEO requirements, which TYPO3 offers without installing any extra extensions.

These requirements are:

- Page keywords and page description:

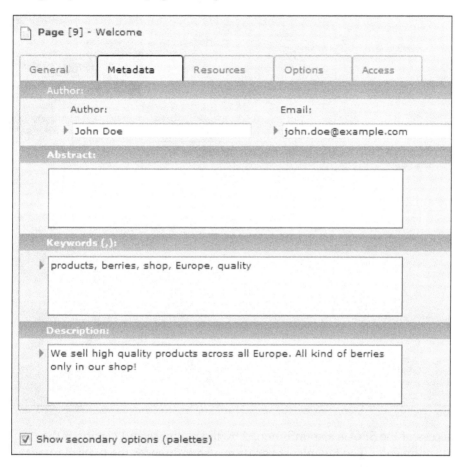

- Content elements in records (for example, "Text w/image")—title for content element, alternative text, and title for images:

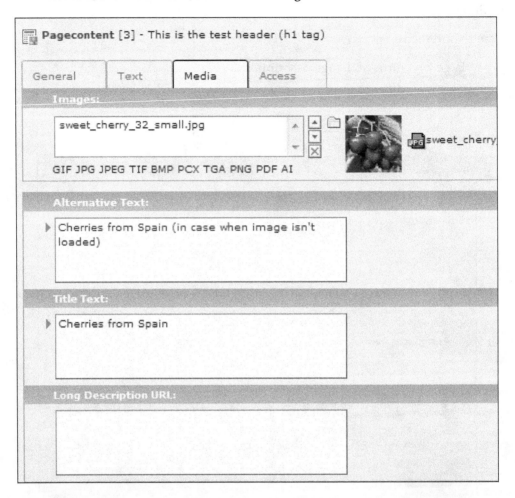

The success of the SEO is also influenced by the neatness and clarity of the programming code. The technical execution also influences the overall quality and usability of a website.

The solutions provided by Google

Google sorts the search results according to the rating of a web page and according to the correspondence to keywords. As Google is the most popular search engine on the Internet, it provides various technical solutions for effective SEO.

One such solution is adding your web page to Google: `http://www.google.com/addurl`

You don't need to add all the pages of your online shop; you only need to add the most characteristic one and those which contain useful information for the visitors.

The recognition of the website by Google can be improved by creating a **Sitemap** file and informing the Google system about this file. This file ensures the recognition of all the pages of a website. If the site map file is not used, it is possible that some of the website's URLs will not be added to Google and thus they will not be found. Google uses the `Sitemap` file (which can be manually created in XML format) to analyse the structure of your website and to index the website's sections more comprehensively. This is an important factor for ensuring that the web page will be found according to certain keywords also in the future.

The `Sitemap` file enlists the sections of your website. The first level categories have to be shown first. The refresh time has to be around an hour. The sublevels have to be shown afterwards. With each level, the refresh time of the web page has to be reduced, since search engines (for example, Google) index web pages beginning with the index page and not with any of the categories. We also made a small `Sitemap` file for our shop, which can serve as an example of which information should be included in this file.

A text file was created and saved with an extension `.xml`. At the beginning of the file, the following must be written:

```
<?xml version="1.0" encoding="UTF-8"?>

<urlset xmlns="http://www.sitemaps.org/schemas/sitemap/0.9">
```

We made entries for addresses of each web page by using a tag `<loc>`. This is an obligatory tag in creating a `Sitemap` file. A `Sitemap` file can also contain entries about the section's last time of modification (tag `<lastmod>`), about the frequency of modifications (tag `<changefreq>`), and about the priority of these modifications (tag `<priority>`), which shows the importance of specific modifications:

```
<url>
    <loc>http://www.yourdomain.com/</loc>
    <lastmod>2009-11-05</lastmod>
    <changefreq>monthly</changefreq>
     <priority>0.7</priority>
</url>
```

At the end of the text file, this should be written:

```
</urlset>
```

Upload the `Sitemap` file on the server of your online shop and inform Google about this file by adding the following line in a file `robots.txt` (for more about this, see: `http://www.robotstxt.org/faq.html`):

```
Sitemap: http://www.yourdomain.com/sitemap.xml
```

The position of this line in the file `robots.txt` is according to your preferences. The `Sitemap` file will provide information about your website not only to the Google search system, but also to any other search system on the Internet that recognizes the `Sitemap` protocol.

Creating a `Sitemap` file manually is recommended for small websites, provided the information is not modified frequently. For larger projects, the option of automatic creation of `Sitemap` files must be used.

We prefer using the TYPO3 extension called "seo_basics" (Basic SEO Features) in order to automatically create the `sitemap.xml` file. This extension is easy to use and it also provides such functions as adding keywords to the web pages.

Extension Manager

Extension: **Basic SEO Features** (seo_basics)

CURRENT STATUS:

The extension is installed (loaded and running)!
Click here to remove the extension:

CONFIGURATION:

(Notice: You may need to clear the cache after the configuration of the extension. This is re

Enable features

Enable the Google XML Sitemap [xmlSitemap]
This enables the Sitemap used for Google, available under www.yourdomain.com/s
☑

Enable the HTML Source Formatter [sourceFormatting]
Does nice indention to the HTML output of your website.
☑

Update

To install this TYPO3 extension, select **Ext Manager** from the left menu of the BE panel. Then select the **Import Extensions** function. Enter the name of the necessary extension in the search field — in our case, type **seo_basics** — and click on the **search** button. Import the extension by clicking on the **Import** button and then install the extension. This will create new tables and you will access extra options.

Next, switch to the Template module and edit your template. Add the static template to the page (**Includes** tab) and then save the changes:

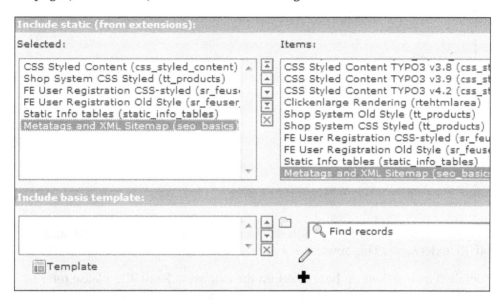

Finally, add the TypoScript configuration in the **Setup** field of the template. This will generate the `sitemap.xml` file:

```
page.headerData.776 < plugin.tx_seobasics
```

Note that the code in this image does not have the beginning part "page", since it has to be configured in the TypoScript parameter. The sample code, which is seen before this, has to be added outside the "page" parameter.

```
Setup:
[global]

page.config.index_enable = 1


# PAGE START
#-------------------------------------------------
    page = PAGE
    page {

    headerData.776 < plugin.tx_seobasics

# SEARCH
#-------------------------------------------------
    config.index_enable = 1


# HEAD DATA - keywords and description
```

Also, note that this TYPO3 extension works with the support of RealURL and CoolURL extensions. This simulates a static document—`sitemap.xml`.

For detailed instructions on how to set up the extension RealURL, please refer to the TYPO3 extension manual: `http://typo3.org/documentation/document-library/extension-manuals/realurl/current/`.

A comprehensive resource with examples of finished RealURL configurations is available on the TYPO3 Wiki page: `http://wiki.typo3.org/index.php/RealURL`

Quick steps for successful SEO

Several steps can be identified for the successful adaptation of SEO for your online shop. The first step is putting effort into defining the keywords and creating the content.

As the degree of specialization of the industry increases, one must do more research on the keywords. This research will determine the subsequent fortunes or misfortunes of your optimization. The best way to do the research is to use the Google Adwords campaign.

Before that, it is a good idea to look up the related and the most relevant keywords with the help of a keyword research tool, for example, Google Keyword Tool (`https://adwords.google.com/select/KeywordToolExternal`).

Since the exact content of a web page is one of the key elements of SEO, the chosen keywords have to be used to create the content. Every new page receives a certain ranking in the Google PageRank, and as the number of pages in a site increases, the stronger the website becomes in terms of SEO. The most important activity of internal optimization (and of SEO in general) is creating new content. The website not only has to be effective but also has to be actualized continuously, and its content has to be updated and extended.

The next step is dealing with the tag line and the description of the page. The title tag influences the compliance of the web page with the searched word or phrase. But the title tag is even more important when the visitor clicks on the search results. For example, the third page in the Google search results, provided it has a successful title tag, can be more attractive to the potential visitor than the first page in the search results, which has a less successful title tag or does not have it at all.

The description (unlike the title tag) does not influence the position of the web page in the search results, but it does influence the choice of the visitor, who is guided not only by title but also by the description of the page. The few lines of description have to attract the visitor's attention, tell them about the content of the page, and also suggest clicking on the link.

The third important step for SEO is links. Precisely, the links are at the centre of external optimization. Yet, just as important is the web page's internal structure of the links. The links have to be created from less important pages to more important pages. The external resources have to link not only to the main page, but also to other less important pages. Currently, there are very many possibilities to generate automatic links (social networks, different RSS services, and so on). Thus there is no need to wait for links from external pages owned by somebody else.

A link is very important, but is much more important when it comes with anchor text. It has to be noted that visitors consider not only the anchor text of the link, but also the content in its proximity. Thus the links that come from a site of the same topic as your web page will be more relevant.

Summary

Search Engine Optimization is an important activity to make a web page effective and profitable. Your SEO can be more effective if your target audience is the population of a certain country. The optimal SEO requirements can be fulfilled in the course of time along with developing the popularity of your online shop and with traditional advertising activities. For the best SEO result, it is necessary to include several aspects, for example, creating the content of the website that corresponds to the goals of the website and the availability of products.

In the next chapter, we will describe the most important aspects for managing and marketing the site.

10
Managing and Marketing Your Site

This chapter covers the most important aspects of managing and marketing a website. Managing an online shop and the relevant marketing activities are the most important components for ensuring the smooth functioning of the online shop and they also pave the way for further development of your business. The topics covered in this chapter are:

- Effective options for shop content views
- Discount, campaign, and the use of different activities
- Support

By the end of this chapter, you should know the common methods of managing and marketing the online shop.

The important aspects of management

"E-Commerce" (electronic commerce) is the service of transfer of goods or payments over global information networks. This includes not only interactive transactions but also specific marketing activities, research of market potential, keeping up relationship with customers and consumers, as well as a flow of corporate documentation. Thus e-Commerce is a complex concept, yet every transaction includes a transfer of electronic data.

In this book, we have examined various technical and practical issues that can help you to create your own online shop on the basis of TYPO3 CMS. But, with the development of e-Commerce, there are more and more online shops that offer various goods. Therefore, you must not only pay attention to the technical development of your online shop, from placing it on a server, to integration of the payment system, to security issues, and of course, to the goods themselves, but you must also know how to make your online shop popular and thus profitable.

The global development in economics and business predicts that e-Commerce services will become even more popular. Thus an online shop is a good way to sell goods and services in terms of profit per investment.

E-Commerce increases the efficiency of trade in the following ways:

- The transaction costs decrease
- The consumer costs of finding the needed goods decrease
- The competition increases
- A specific client strategy is formed
- The efficiency of business process management increases

The potential customers have the technologies (Internet access, computers, credit cards) to choose the needed goods and to make payment online. This saves time, as it is possible to see the offers of many goods or services over a short period of time. It is possible to purchase goods from other cities internationally.

The business, however, can optimize its costs of sale by, for instance, offering the goods only in an online shop. E-shop has a great potential for growth by offering the goods to customers from various target groups or from various countries. Yet, the main goal of an online shop is still making profit.

The management of an online shop includes using the same marketing methods as in traditional businesses. Yet, a number of new notions have to be considered — e-mail marketing, search engine optimization (SEO) activities, context advertisement, banners, affiliates marketing, among others.

Likewise, the competition is different in e-Commerce. Every business, which offers similar goods or services online, immediately becomes the competitor of your online shop. The situation is complicated because if, for example, your online shop offers berries to customers in Europe, every online vendor of berries for the same group of customers becomes your competitor.

The physical location of your shop or warehouse is less important than in the case of traditional shops, where the location closer to the potential customer is immensely important for business success.

When establishing an online shop, one should prepare a strategic business plan; one must identify potential risks and threats and scenarios to avoid those dangers. Likewise, necessary calculations of prices, discounts, and other things have to be prepared.

There are two general ways of how to plan the online shop. One way is creating a detailed business plan while the second is creating a strategic plan. The choice of either way depends on the availability of initial investment and the availability of time for preparation.

Your experience in dealing with the specific goods that would be sold through your online shop is crucial. Basically, there are two ways:

- You have some prior experience in, for example, selling berries
- You do not have any prior experience in selling berries

If the first way is the case, you will know, based on your experience, a lot about berries — the various kinds of berries and the details about storing and transporting them. You will also know about the producers of berries, the quality they offer, and the terms and conditions of their selling contracts. This experience will help you greatly when opening an online shop. You may also have some experience in selling. Maybe you have a fruit business that is not available on the Internet. Again, this is an advantage for your potential e-business.

The second scenario means that you do not have any prior experience in selling berries and no knowledge whatsoever about this product. Maybe you have some other business experience or maybe you have sold something online. If this is the case, opening a large-scale online berry shop includes much more business risks.

If you have never sold berries before, it is recommended that you do some test sales before you go for a large scale business. Thus the risks will be reduced by gaining some information about the market and the customers.

In some cases, it is useful to set up a test web page in order to explore the demand of your goods. Thus the initial costs of your large scale business will also be reduced. Create, for example, an online shop that offers various kinds of berries.

During the test sales, you must follow the statistics of visitors and purchases. Your test online shop also has to be advertised, and the customers have to be informed about the production. If there is a stable demand over a certain period of time, you can begin a large-scale sale and plan greater investments for creating an online shop.

After the test phase, you might learn that some kinds of berries are demanded more than others. Thus you will know which berries will be sold at larger volumes.

Sometimes it is a good option to sell goods on demand. Yet, creating and developing such an online shop is much harder because potential customers like to purchase goods that are available immediately rather than wait for a long delivery.

Certainly, such business models are feasible if you communicate the benefits of such an approach to your customers—for example, that the berries will be picked after placing the orders, thus keeping them fresh for a longer period of time.

The next step is planning your business in general and planning the specific activities for creating an effective and technically well-developed online shop. In addition to deciding to sell certain kinds of berries, you must also determine the main directions of development: this is the business mission, vision, and the values. These form the so-called "business philosophy".

The mission of your berry business might be, for example:

- To improve the health and condition of people by offering them berries of the highest quality!

The vision might be:

- To be the leading berry shop in Europe!

When defining a mission and vision, one must keep in mind that these are not just plain words or just an obligatory step. Indeed, it is possible to develop an online shop without the "philosophical" side of it, but in the long run, the mission and vision show the way for the management of the business as well as for the employees. These formulations motivate heading in the right direction for achieving the main goals of the business.

Our mission and vision define the stand the company takes that health is a value and that the berries offered by the online shop stimulate the health and well-being of people.

Thus the values underlying the popularization of the online shop might be as follows:

- Health
- Feeling of comfort
- Joy of living
- Responsibility

Every business idea has two initial challenges:

- How to create an organization that would make profit
- How to create the specific approach to attract the customers and to face competition

Arguably, the main component in the process of making the profit is the product. If, for example, there is no online berry shop, two explanations are possible: either there is no demand for such goods or the producers of berries use different channels of distribution.

The demand for a product, as mentioned before, can be identified by the test sales.

If the test sales show that there is some demand for the berries, then you have certain advantages if you are the first one to set up an online berry shop. But this is until other competitors appear.

But if the berries are sold in online shops, you must create your specific approach to attract customers and ensure the competitiveness of your online shop.

If you plan on increasing the sales in future, then your initial strategy might be a good basis for the development of your brand. This also means development of your online shop (and your business) on the international level.

In the case of an online shop as a form of business, the main aspects when creating a profitable enterprise are:

- Attitude
- Time and costs
- The specifics of market and target customers
- Requirements for the online shop
- Technical requirements

Creating an online shop is an interesting and exciting process. But it also has to be done responsibly, because it is the basis of you business success.

Before creating an online shop, the time and especially the financial resources have to be considered. This is the advantage of TYPO3 CMS because it makes it possible to decrease the costs of technical development while maintaining functionality and flexibility of the web pages.

Before opening an online shop, it is necessary to identify the target customer and the target geographical area. These considerations determine the visual, functional, and technical requirements of the online shop.

Here are some other considerations before starting an online shop:

- The product to be sold
- What information will be present in the page and how often will it be updated
- The applicable legislation
- The opening hours of the online shop (usually it is 24 hours a day, 7 days a week, but there can be exceptions)
- The type of sales — retail, wholesale, or both

These considerations will determine the technical requirements of your planned online shop.

In relation to the online purchases, an important question to be decided is whether the visitors of the online shop will have to register. On the one hand, it is recommended not to force the client to register, as it is an extra inconvenience, but on the other hand, the information about the registered customers can be useful in marketing activities. Therefore, it is a good idea to make the registration optional.

An important technical aspect is automatized operation of the online shop. This decreases the costs and ensures that the purchases made in your online shop are not dependant on any other factor than the wish of the consumer to buy the goods.

And certainly, the most important aspect for the future of an online shop is its popularization and marketing activities.

When planning the advertisement of your online shop, the aforementioned business strategy and values have to be considered. The advertisement must generally follow the main goal of the popularization — be it the introduction of a new product in the market or the popularization of an already established online shop.

The popularization activities also have to react to the actions of competitors. Sometimes an intuition might be helpful when quick and effective solutions have to be found.

The suggestions for how to popularize an online shop can be divided as follows:

- The visual aspects of a shop
- Fostering customer loyalty
- Identification of the main risks
- Popularization of an online shop — marketing.

The visual aspects of an online shop

The design of your online shop must be attractive so that it builds trust in your visitors. An online shop is one of your company's visual elements, and therefore it has to include the colors, logos, and typeface of your company.

It is necessary to ensure that the chosen design allows for a quick loading of the page and that the page is easy to understand. This builds on the principle that a sophisticated multi-functional system (an online shop is such a system) should appear to be "easy" and simple.

The main principles of the visual aspects of online shop are the following:

1. The design of an online shop should be easily scalable — the quantity of goods can change over time, it can increase while some categories of goods might be abandoned.

2. The catalog of goods should be well-structured so that the customers can find the product they are looking for by browsing through just one or two subcategories (a search area is a good option too).

3. A place should be planned for various information (special sales, discounts, a place for banners of business partners, and so on).

4. It is a good idea to decorate the online shop with the themes of some holidays or days of celebration. This would create the feeling that there is "somebody behind the design".

Let's discuss each principle in more detail. First, templates can be subdivided into two base groups:

*   Fixed width templates — the width of the templates is usually fixed at 950-990 pixels breadth-wise
*   Fluid templates

Fixed width templates are used most often, whereas fluid templates are rarely used. It is because creating a fluid template is more complicated for a web page developer.

`http://www.w3schools.com/browsers/browsers_display.asp`, you can see that the users' display resolution is growing. Most web page visitors are using a screen size of 1024x768 pixels or more.

Fixed width templates affect the comfortable reviewing of web pages. Using fixed templates can lead to a situation where the web page is difficult to review. For example, if a web page visitor is browsing your web page on a 21.5" iMac PC with a resolution of 1920x1080 pixels and your web page has a fixed width of 850 pixels, it will be difficult to view the page comfortably.

Fluid templates expand or collapse with the width of the screen, whereas fixed templates always stay the same width.

Also, we would like to supplement the main principles with some simple examples. First of all, you should remember that your web page may grow in the future so it is useful to leave some room for growth in the web page design.

You can see an example of a design in the following screenshot where there isn't place for any content to be added:

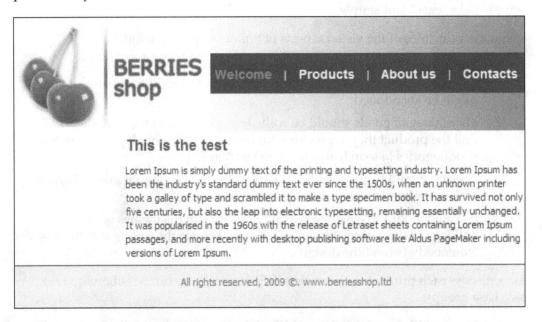

As you can see in this example, if you need to add one more menu item, you will have to change the design or add an extra line for the menu.

We recommend dividing the menu into several parts—a menu for bases like **About us** and **Contact**, and a menu for sections that may grow, like **Catalogue**. Also, you can foresee that submenus will be located, for example, across the left part of the web page, so you can increase the submenus and keep the design of your web page.

Similarly, it is not good to leave a lot of empty space in you online shop design like you see in the following example:

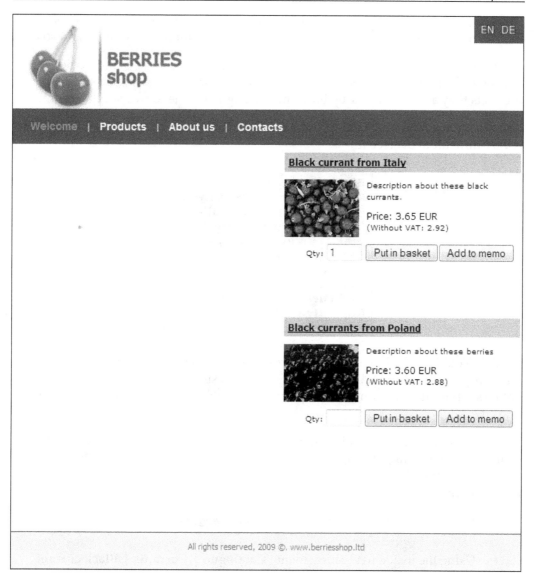

This online shop looks empty, which isn't good for representation.

The best way to present your website is to place the content and leave a blank area in a shapely manner. You will have to foresee where you will need to add more content, menus, and other elements, and which parts of your online shop will stay constant for a long time.

Don't forget to leave some place for marketing activities in your design, such as information about discount campaigns, information about new products, and so on.

The next principle is the structure of your catalogue. As we mentioned previously, a catalog should be well-structured. It is important that the customers can find the products they are looking for by browsing through just one to two subcategories.

You can see the following example of a catalog menu that isn't structured well, so it is very difficult to oversee it:

```
Black currants
Black currant from Italy
Black currant from Holland
Black currant from Poland
Black currant from Spain
Red currants
Red currant from Italy
Red currant from Holland
Red currant from Poland
Red currant from Spain
```

Visitors would need to concentrate a lot to find **Red currants**. We recommend laying out a large catalog or a catalog with many obvious subsections. If a visitor visits your online shop for the first time, it is important that he finds the necessary product and finds it easily.

If you are marketing your online shop as a "good" online shop, visitors should feel comfortable navigating through sections, subsections, and web page content. It is very important that visitors don't feel lost in your site. You can use simple methods to ensure this:

- Using URLs: `http://www.yourshop.com/eng/catalogue/currants/blackcurrantsitaly`

- Using the inside navigation menu: **Catalogue | Currants | Black currant**

For ease, oversee the structure of your catalogue hierarchically, as you see in the following image:

Black currants
> **Black currant from Italy**
> **Black currant from Holland**
> **Black currant from Poland**
> **Black currant from Spain**
> **Black currant from Spain 2**

Red currants
> **Red currant from Italy**
> **Red currant from Holland**
> **Red currant from Poland**

And it is even better if you don't use the same words repeatedly. In our example, it is words **Black/Red currant from**. To solve it, you can use a different technique; for example, add some explanation to the catalogue and structure it like in the following image:

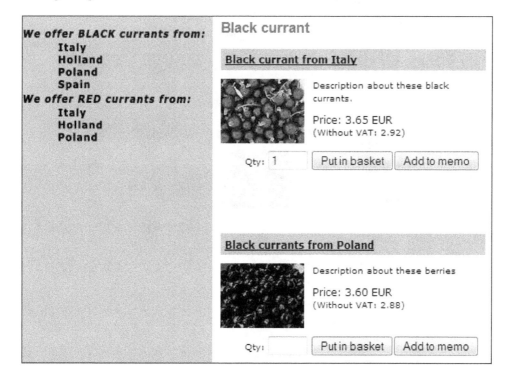

The third principle is that, in your website, space should be planned for various information. You should plan areas for information about special sales, discounts, and a place for banners of business partners, among others. The easiest way to include all the necessary areas in web page design is that you plan base marketing activities before creating your online shop.

In the example below, we can see that there is no place for any banners any more in this design:

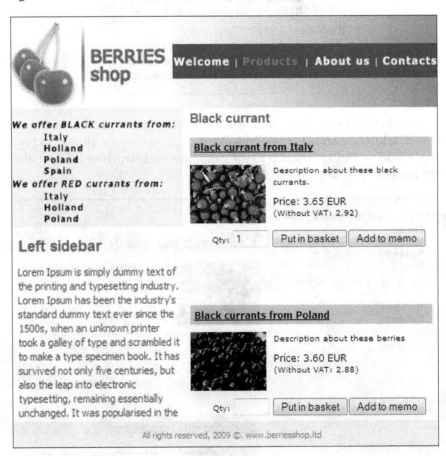

If you know that you will use special sales and information about discounts for marketing your site, you should foresee the area for it, like in the following image:

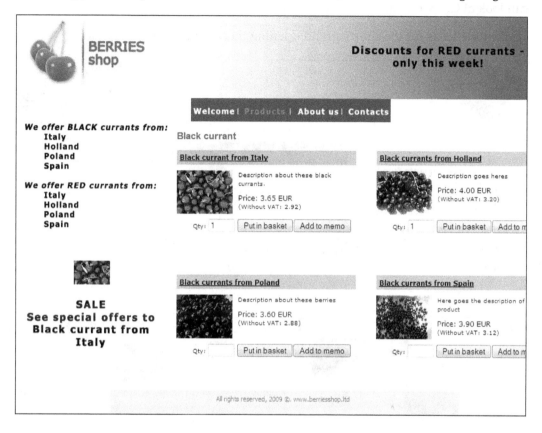

You can highlight your campaign by using:

- SALE
- Attention!
- Only this week…
- Special offer…
- Use your chance…
- Discounts…

The fourth principle is to decorate the online shop with the themes of some holidays or days of celebration. We will create some examples to see how your online shop can look at Christmas and on the shop's grand opening.

Look at the ideas for the shop's grand opening theme in the following image:

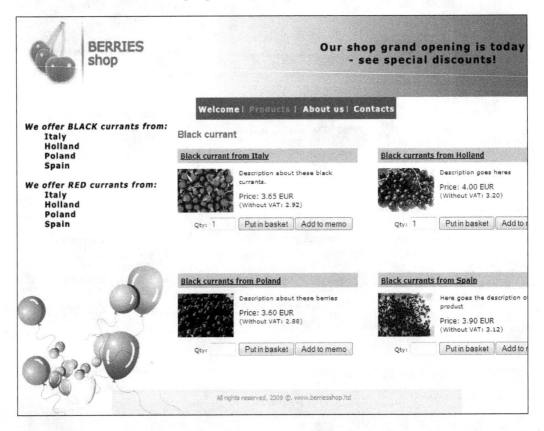

You could use just one element to update your online shop design. Also, you could use several elements, change colors, or add some textual information and greetings for your visitors. We recommend using celebrations to market your online shop and to give special discounts to your customers.

You can set up a "special" package on celebrations, for example:

- Special currant pack at Christmas
- Red currants for a summer party
- Poland currants double pack

Use your imagination and see the results of these sales, and you will learn what is best for your customers.

Look at the ideas for a Christmas theme in the following image:

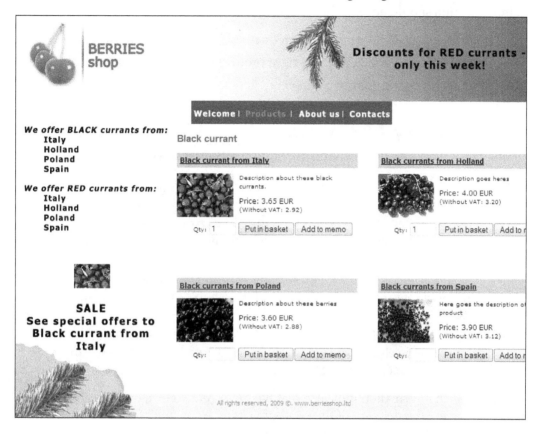

You could choose celebrations according to what matches your online shop profile. Don't use each and every celebration if it is not necessary.

With these modifications, you keep your online shop alive, dynamic, and interesting. You can find links to external developer resources on TYPO3 at: `http://typo3.org/documentation/other-resources/`.

Fostering customer loyalty

It is important for the owners of an online shop to build customer loyalty. Therefore, the information in the online shop, the manager of the business, and public communication should answer the following questions:

- What is the guarantee that the product will be delivered?
- What is the guarantee that the right product will be delivered?
- What will be the quality of delivered goods?

The delivery of goods

In order to inform the customer, it is useful to create a section of the page where the following information is laid out:

- The delivery of goods — the timing and means
- The cost of delivery, depending on the distance of delivery and the weight of the product (usually, the cost of delivery is not included in the price of the product)
- The terms and conditions of returning a product (depending on the legislation, it might be mandatory, but the shop can offer this as an extra option)
- The way of handling disputes and whom to contact in such cases (the person in charge should know the legal details and also have an authority to act on behalf of the online shop)

Providing such information indicates that the management of the online shop is willing to secure the delivery of the goods, inform the customers about the process of delivery, and help the client in handling disputes.

Of course, it is not possible to predict all of the information that should be available on your page, but as the shop will be operational, this will emerge.

The information about delivery and returning goods can have a reference to the applicable legislation. This will indicate that the management of the shop knows the legislation and that it is considered important — all this will increase the trust in your online shop.

Delivering the right product

One of the ways to ensure that the visitor of the shop buys the right goods is prompting the customer to confirm the selected goods (in our case, berries) before a visitor makes the payment:

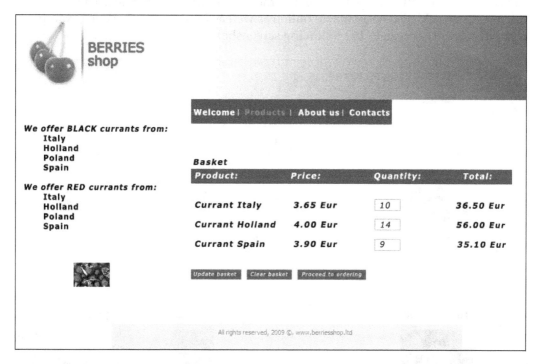

If the purchase is made by a registered user, it is recommended that a confirmation e-mail be sent to the customer. This e-mail should contain information about the purchase (the price and the quantity of the goods).

If the customer has made a mistake, such e-mail of confirmation gives him/her a chance to contact the representatives of the online shop who can then correct this mistake.

The quality of goods

To convince the customer about the quality of the goods, it is possible to refer to certificates or documentation that confirm the quality.

This information can be displayed next to the description of the goods. These documents should also be available online as well as for download (as, for example, a pdf document) as seen in the following screenshot:

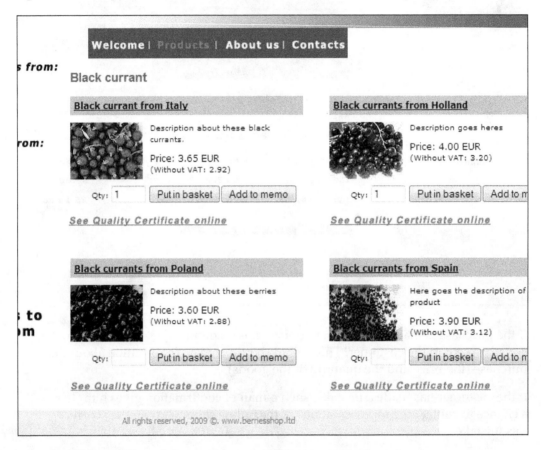

If you sell the goods (say, the berries) as the middleman, you must consider the complaints of customers. Sometimes it might be required to switch the suppliers of the goods because the quality of goods influences your reputation—the customers will not make return purchases and will spread negative information about you to others.

The quality of goods should be monitored persistently. The range of available goods should also be adjusted when such a need arises.

Customer loyalty for the online shop is gained gradually. But at the time of establishing an online shop, one can also make sure that the right information is available. This will foster loyalty and will stimulate the customer to return to the online shop again and again.

When creating an online shop, one should ensure that the system works without faults — all the functions work correctly, and the online shop is available 24/7. Likewise, it is important to enlarge the number of visitors to the online shop to increase its popularity.

The service of online purchases means that the customer will be able to get some online support.

There are several ways that the visitor to an online shop can contact its employees:

- E-mail
- Phone
- Fax
- Skype
- An online contact form
- Online chat
- A video call

It is not recommended to use all these means of contact, but rather choose three or four methods that are more relevant to your target audience.

The statistics of which means of communication the customers use to contact the online shop can be useful to consider the usefulness of some of these methods.

When choosing the means of communication, it is necessary to remember that there are some people who like to ask questions "silently" — they will use e-mail or online contact form. Some people, however, prefer live communication — the phone or Skype. With this in mind, it is recommended to combine various means of communication.

Main risks

One of the main threats for an online shop is for the content of the web page to be any of the following:

- Irrelevant
- Insufficient
- Incomprehensible

When creating the information, which will be available to potential customers, it should be noted that all of the information should be evaluated from the customer's point of view — the information should tell which goods are sold on the online shop and what qualities these goods have.

In an ordinary shop, the customer has several ways to check the goods.
The customer can:

- Touch the product
- See the product (quality, freshness)
- Taste the product (only in some cases, of course)
- Speak with the shopkeeper
- Read the manuals and supporting documentation of the goods

Choosing a product — if it is purchased for the first time — takes a lot of time.
An online shop generally saves time that the customer spends while getting to the ordinary shop, but the amount of time spent choosing the product might be the same.

Therefore, the information on the online shop must be created so that it is comprehensible, easy to perceive, useful, and in the right quantity.

Thus, relevant information can stimulate the customer to choose the online shop instead of the ordinary shop to make a purchase. But an online shop has some extra advantages that an ordinary shop does not have:

- Lower prices
- Delivery of goods
- Longer opening hours

The visual material (photos) should also be chosen carefully. If there are no photos of the available goods (or the photos are very small or of poor quality), this might lead the customer to think that:

- The seller does not have these goods as she cannot take photos of the goods
- The seller is superficial about the goods

Both cases work against the reputation of the seller.

Replacing a part of the necessary information with video of some details about the online shop is becoming more and more popular. The length of the video material should not exceed 5-7 minutes.

Such videos are an alternative to the written text and they also do not take large resources or time to create. There is no need to use professional equipment—one can use, for example, the video recording functions of an ordinary PC.

Also, the video material should be comprehensible and related to the goods (and their qualities) that are sold on the online shop.

If video material is used, it has to be supplemented with textual and other visual information. Some of the customers might not wish to (or cannot due to technical problems) watch the video. Therefore, the necessary information shouldn't just be on the video.

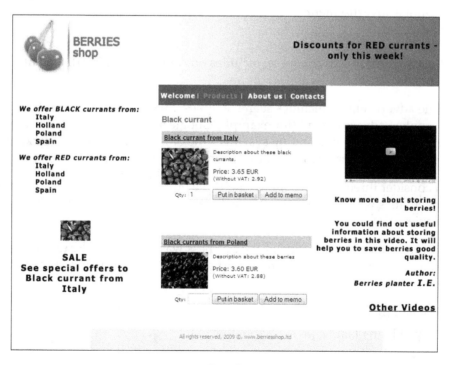

Also, from the perspective of SEO, too much video material is not recommended. The video should be supplemented with additional information:

- The title of the video
- Short outline
- Author
- The reason for watching this video, for example, **Know more about storing berries!**

The image above shows how a video material is supplemented with information about the berries available on the online shop.

Also, from the point of view of copyrights, the video is less likely to be copied. Certainly, the information in the video can be transcribed and used for other purposes, but it is much harder than with written text or images.

Popularization of an online shop

To popularize your online shop, you can choose in several possible ways—the one that fits your target customers and your marketing budget. The advertisement can be divided into large groups:

- Online advertisement
- Offline advertisement

The offline advertisement, of course, includes outdoor media, advertisement in radio, printed media, TV, booklets, and so on.

The online advertisement includes search engines, catalogs, banners, sending e-mails, context advertisement (for example, Google adwords) and advertisement in sales catalogs, and web page rating systems. One of the latest trends is working with the target audience in various thematic forums and blogs.

We will consider three possible online and three offline marketing activities. The aim of these activities will be informing the customers about the new online shop, which offers berries.

As the "philosophical" conception of the business was developed, let us choose some keywords on which to base the advertisement. The basic values of our berry business are:

- Health (fresh, tasty)
- Joy of living (smile, joy)

As the online advertisement activities, we choose the following:

- Work with target audience
- Adwords
- Catalogues

To attract potential customers, the first thing to do is create relevant information in our online shop—as mentioned before, it has to be both textual and visual (images, photos, and/or videos).

The next step is finding out which websites in your region (city, state) would be the most suitable for advertising your online shop.

Before spreading the information, you must know about what will happen within the following month:

- Will there be sales of goods and when will they be?
- When will new kinds of berries be available?
- Will there be some special offers (for, say, regular customers) and when will they be?

Working with the target audience

We might choose to popularize our online shop in such ways as:

- Registering on several of the most popular forums for fruit growers of your region
- Creating our own Twitter blog
- Informing the mass media about our activities

You should post only professional opinions in the forums—about various kinds of berries, about storing berries, about producers, and so on. You must gain a reputation as an expert in such forums—this will indicate that your online shop wants to be considered an expert in the field.

A good way of getting noticed is to star new topics and react on older posts.

Also, reading the forums regularly lets you know what people think about fruit-growing, about berries, using berries, and growing and selling berries.

For posting short messages, micro blog Twitter (`http://www.twitter.com`) is more appropriate. You can post information about the opening of your online shop, about sales and special offers, as well your opinion about the various issues that would interest your followers, because Twitter offers the option to follow a certain user to know the latest news.

When using Twitter, it is important to remember that it is a tool for the development of your business, though others might find it funny or exciting. Therefore, you should carefully choose the words when posting a message. This blog represents your corporate identity. It a useful tool for communicating with your potential customers.

For more information about using Twitter as a business tool, refer to **A special guide here**: `http://business.twitter.com/twitter101`

Another option for publicity (which is free) is creating press releases. These should contain useful and important information about the main activities of your business. This tool should be used when opening your online shop and when informing people about some special sales or offers.

The above described means of popularization of your business are free. Yet, it takes some time to prepare the information. Once you publish some information, you should monitor what influence it has on the number of visits to your page and on the number of purchases.

You should state that you use Twitter or that you have prepared a press release in the web page of your online shop:

Such well-prepared and planned work with information should bring popularity to your online shop. This will bring new customers, higher sales, and more profit.

Adwords

Another way to advertise your online shop is Adwords. This channel of advertisement is quite effective and it also allows you to plan the cost of advertisement.

The largest provider of such a service is Google Adwords. It offers placing advertisements, and choosing the keywords that are related to the product of your online shop—in our case, berries. You can relate those keywords with the ones you used in SEO (see Chapter 9). But you can also choose different keywords and synonyms. The advertisement will be displayed when people search for these keywords.

The efficiency of Adwords is related to various aspects:

- Your advertisement will be seen by those people who search for specific keywords

- There is the possibility to click on your advertisement to know more about the product and even to buy your berries

- It is possible to narrow down the audience of your advertisement, not only by keywords but also geographically

For example, let us calculate the cost of keywords (using `https://adwords.google.com`) that can be used to create the following advertisement in Google Adwords:

- Fresh berries

Keywords	Estimated Ad Position ⑦	Estimated Avg. CPC ⑦	Match Type: ⑦ Broad ⌄
Keywords related to term(s) entered - sorted by relevance ⑦			
fresh berry	1 - 3	€0.67	Add ⌄
fresh berries recipes	1 - 3	€0.05	Add ⌄
fresh berries dessert	1 - 3	€0.05	Add ⌄
freezing fresh berries	1 - 3	€0.05	Add ⌄
fresh berries	1 - 3	€0.82	Add ⌄

- Berries online

Keywords	Estimated Ad Position ⑦	Estimated Avg. CPC ⑦	Match Type: ⑦ Broad ⌄
Keywords related to term(s) entered - sorted by relevance ⑦			
berry online	1 - 3	€0.05	Add ⌄
berries online	1 - 3	€2.87	Add ⌄

- Tasty berries

Keywords	Estimated Ad Position ⑦	Estimated Avg. CPC ⑦	Broad ⌄
Keywords related to term(s) entered - sorted by relevance ⑦			
berry tasty muffins	1 - 3	€0.05	Add ⌄
tasty berries	1 - 3	€0.05	Add ⌄

Although the phrase **tasty berries** will cost you less per click, other data also has to be considered. For example, out of these three options, the phrase **tasty berries** has been searched the most — 12,100 times per month. Therefore, it would be useful to use these keywords when creating an Adwords advertisement.

The text of the advertisement could be as follows:

- Choose tasty berries
- Buy fresh berries online
- Become healthy and happy
- www.yourinternetshop.com

To find out more about Google Adwords and to register for it, visit adwords.google.com.

Catalogues

Another additional option is creating catalogues that contain information about the kinds of berries, their prices, and producers. Descriptions and visual material should also be included in the catalogues.

Such catalogues can be placed in your online shop. The customers should have an option to download all the information for browsing, even in the offline mode.

Likewise, such catalogues can be placed in the web pages of your partners who are not your competitors. For example:

- In the web page of a pharmacy
- In the online shop of vegetables
- In the portal for young parents

The availability of such catalogues will create an interest for potential target customers, the popularity of your web page will increase, and the information about your online shop will spread.

We will also consider the following methods of offline advertisement:

- Flyers
- Advertisement in radio
- Advertisement in magazines

If online advertisement has the benefit of targeting those customers who use the Internet (which is crucial for an online shop), then offline advertisement can reach those who use the Internet less often but who, nevertheless, are your potential customers.

Flyers

Using flyers is a very cost-effective means of advertisement for a new business. A flyer is a small leaflet that is very often colorful. Flyers are usually handed out to promote some product or service.

Using flyers can be an effective way to advertise and to attract attention to a specific product or event. On the other hand, flyers can also spoil the image of the advertised product. Therefore, some considerations have to be made when preparing flyers.

The design of the flyers has to be adjusted to the forthcoming event so that it quickly delivers the message to the customer. Thus, the number of people who consider this information would increase.

Depending on what is being advertised and who is the target audience, the flyers can be image-building or informative. The latter would contain information about the product, its price, and advantages.

The main task of a flyer is to influence the choice of the potential customer.

Flyers are a cheap and easy-to-distribute channel of advertising. The text on the flyer has to be short and concise. As in a good advertisement, the title of the flyer has to have a gimmick, and the text has to describe the benefits of the product. Depending on the target customers, the flyers are usually distributed in public places—shopping centers, bus stops, on streets, in parks, and so on.

The message of the flyers should be no more than 10 words long. If possible, use symbols. The message should be structured as follows:

- What is it?
- Where is it?
- How much does it cost?
- Where can I find additional information?

Such flyers can be used, for example, to stimulate interest in your online shop even before its opening. You can urge the customer to visit the web page on the specific date of opening of your shop. In this case, however, you should not start your advertisement too early and you also should make sure that the web page contains the "under construction" information.

Radio

You can also use radio advertisements to reach potential customers who would be interested in buying berries online. Radio advertisement is very effective; it can reach a much larger audience.

This type of advertisement costs more, but if the text is well-formed, it is possible to reach a much larger audience and persuade them to visit your online shop.

Advertisement in magazines

Thematic magazines are also an effective way to reach your target customer. Those potential customers who have chosen to read a thematic magazine about, for example, cookery, healthy lifestyle, or food, have already, in a sense, taken a large step towards you.

As we know, advertisements in magazines can be large or small. The influence of the advertisement has to be weighted against your financial resources. There is no sense in placing a very small advertisement just for the sake of placing an advertisement— the advertisement works only if it can be noticed.

Among other means of advertisement, the affiliates marketing, the banner agencies, and the price information portals should be mentioned. For more information about these, refer to specialized literature or search the Web.

All these examples were meant just as suggestions or ideas for your advertisement campaigns. Of course, when your online shop becomes a large-scale business, you will hire or consult a marketing expert. But, at the beginning, you will have to get along with just this knowledge, confidence in your ideas, and a creative approach.

These various ways of marketing demand different investment of finances and time. Yet, the main idea behind popularizing your online shop is to provide the potential visitors of the shop with answers to some of these questions:

- Where is it possible to buy what the potential customer is looking for?
- Which online shop has the widest range of various goods and where is the largest choice?

- Which online shop offers the lowest price for the product?
- Which online shop has a specific product?
- Which online shop has the cheapest (or free) delivery?
- Which online shop offers the quickest delivery?
- Which online shop has some special discounts or bonuses?

The popularization of your online shop should include the answers to these questions already in advance. Do remember that the way you organize the purchase of your goods, the delivery, and the communication with the clients will create the overall image of your online shop. If this image is positive, the customer will recommend your shop to his/her friends and may return to it later herself.

The use of online or offline marketing depends on the specific country where you are operating and its market. If you choose to develop a regional business, you will have to consider the tendencies and the specific character of this region.

Equally important is to help the customer to orient in the range of the goods. You can create specific banners containing information about new goods and special deals, as well as about goods that fit some special occasion, and the goods that are discounted or exclusive.

The Internet provides a lot of opportunities—the target audience is relatively easy to reach. At the same time, the most effective channels for communication to the audience have to be found. Only then can an interest in your online shop be created and the customers gain a positive experience. This then will ensure that the customers trust your professionalism, recommend your shop to their friends, and eventually, return to your shop.

Summary

The design of your online shop must be attractive so that it can build trust in your visitors.

It is important for the owners of an online shop to build customer loyalty. It is important to enlarge the number of visitors to the online shop to increase its popularity.

Various ways of marketing demand different investments of finances and time.

Big online shops have departments for each topic mentioned in this chapter. Therefore, this chapter can only be a guide to start with.

Index

N

navigation
  GMENU 92
  HMENU 92
  IMGMENU 92
  menus 92
  TMENU 92

O

online shop
  catalogue hierarchically structure 171-175
  customer loyalty, fostering 176
  inside navigation menu 170
  main risks 180
  popularizing 182
  products, adding to 68- 71
  URLs, using 170
  visual aspects 167-170
  visual aspects, princples 167-170
online shop, popularizing
  adwords 185, 186
  catalogues 186
  flyers 187, 188
  magazines advertisements 188
  ofline advertisement 182
  online advertisement 182
  radio 188
  target audience, working with 183, 184
optimal SEO requirements
  about 152
  Google, solutions 154-158
  page content 154
  page keywords 153
  website content requirements 152, 154
orders processing
  about 107
  extension, setting up 109
  shop_manager extension 108, 109

P

page content
  adding 42-45
  entry fields 45
  TYPO3 minor version update 47
  TYPO3, updating 49

TYPO3, upgrading 46
page module
  about 118
  nodes, switching between 118
  Product record view 119
payment modules 110
payment_paypal extension
  using 115
payments processing
  payment_paypal extension, using 115
  PayPal account, using 115
payment system
  about 55
  options 55
  PayPal system 56
PayPal test account
  merchant account 56
  Pro merchant account 56
  setting up 56-58
PNG format
  benefits 64
product records
  creating 71-74

Q

QuickEdit 118

R

Rich Text Editor extension. *See* RTE extension
risks, online shops
  about 180-182
  advantages 180
  goods, checking 180
RTE extension
  about 136, 137
  rtehtmlarea 136
rtehtmlarea
  about 136
  replacements 136

S

Search Engine Optimization. *See* SEO
searching functionality, TYPO3
  indexed_search extension 100

Thank you for buying
TYPO3 4.2 E-Commerce

About Packt Publishing

Packt, pronounced 'packed', published its first book "*Mastering phpMyAdmin for Effective MySQL Management*" in April 2004 and subsequently continued to specialize in publishing highly focused books on specific technologies and solutions.

Our books and publications share the experiences of your fellow IT professionals in adapting and customizing today's systems, applications, and frameworks. Our solution based books give you the knowledge and power to customize the software and technologies you're using to get the job done. Packt books are more specific and less general than the IT books you have seen in the past. Our unique business model allows us to bring you more focused information, giving you more of what you need to know, and less of what you don't.

Packt is a modern, yet unique publishing company, which focuses on producing quality, cutting-edge books for communities of developers, administrators, and newbies alike. For more information, please visit our website: www.packtpub.com.

About Packt Open Source

In 2010, Packt launched two new brands, Packt Open Source and Packt Enterprise, in order to continue its focus on specialization. This book is part of the Packt Open Source brand, home to books published on software built around Open Source licences, and offering information to anybody from advanced developers to budding web designers. The Open Source brand also runs Packt's Open Source Royalty Scheme, by which Packt gives a royalty to each Open Source project about whose software a book is sold.

Writing for Packt

We welcome all inquiries from people who are interested in authoring. Book proposals should be sent to author@packtpub.com. If your book idea is still at an early stage and you would like to discuss it first before writing a formal book proposal, contact us; one of our commissioning editors will get in touch with you.

We're not just looking for published authors; if you have strong technical skills but no writing experience, our experienced editors can help you develop a writing career, or simply get some additional reward for your expertise.

PUBLISHING

Building Websites with TYPO3

ISBN: 978-1-847191-11-3   Paperback: 208 pages

A practical guide to getting your TYPO3 website up and running fast

1. A practical step-by-step tutorial to creating your TYPO3 website

2. Install and configure TYPO3

3. Master all the important aspects of TYPO3, including the backend, the frontend, content management, and templates

TYPO3 4.3 Multimedia Cookbook

ISBN: 978-1-847198-48-8   Paperback: 228 pages

Over 50 great recipes for effectively managing multimedia content to create an organized web site in TYPO3

1. Create impressive web sites by adding image, video, and audio files to a TYPO3-driven web site and customizing their display

2. Organize you web site by effectively managing your multimedia content in your TYPO3 site

3. Enhance your CMS by adding different processing capabilities such as parsing metadata and converting files to your site

Please check **www.PacktPub.com** for information on our titles

TYPO3: Enterprise Content Management

ISBN: 978-1-904811-41-1   Paperback: 624 pages

The Official TYPO3 Book, written and endorsed by the core TYPO3 Team

1.   Easy-to-use introduction to TYPO3

2.   Design and build content rich extranets and intranets

3.   Learn how to manage content and administrate and extend TYPO3

TYPO3 Extension Development

ISBN: 978-1-847192-12-7   Paperback: 232 pages

Developer's guide to creating feature rich extensions using the TYPO3 API

1.   Covers the complete extension development process from planning and extension generation through development to writing documentation

2.   Includes both front-end and back-end development

3.   Describes TYPO3 areas not covered in the official documentation (such as using AJAX and eID)

Please check **www.PacktPub.com** for information on our titles